MACMILLAN READERS

PRE-INTERMEDIATE LEVEL

THOMAS HARDY

Far From the Madding Crowd

Retold by John Escott

MACMILLAN

MACMILLAN READERS

PRE-INTERMEDIATE LEVEL

Founding Editor: John Milne

The Macmillan Readers provide a choice of enjoyable reading materials for learners of English. The series is published at six levels – Starter, Beginner, Elementary, Pre-intermediate, Intermediate and Upper.

Level Control

Information, structure and vocabulary are controlled to suit the students' ability at each level.

The number of words at each level:

Starter	about 300 basic words
Beginner	about 600 basic words
Elementary	about 1100 basic words
Pre-intermediate	about 1400 basic words
Intermediate	about 1600 basic words
Upper	about 2200 basic words

Vocabulary

Some difficult words and phrases in this book are important for understanding the story. Some of these words are explained in the story, some are shown in the pictures, and others are marked with a number like this: ...[3]. Words with a number are explained in the Glossary at the end of the book.

Answer Keys

Answer Keys for the *Points for Understanding* and *Exercises* sections can be found at www.macmillanenglish.com

Contents

NORTH WESSEX
River Avon
MID-WESSEX
Bristol Channel
Bath
Stonehenge
UPPER WESSEX
OUTER WESSEX
Melchester
SOUTH WESSEX
LOWER WESSEX
Emminster
Chalk-Newton
Norcombe Hill
Weatherbury
Casterbridge
River Frome
Budmouth
The English Channel

A Note About the Author

Thomas Hardy was born on 2nd June, 1840, in the village of Higher Bockhampton. The village is in the county[1] of Dorset, in the south of England.

Thomas's father was a builder and a stonemason – he cut and shaped pieces of stone for building. Thomas's mother loved reading and she owned many books. Thomas was the eldest child. He had a brother and two sisters.

Thomas Hardy went to a good school in Dorchester, the nearest town to his home. He learnt Latin, French, German and Mathematics, as well as Literature, Science and Art.

When he was sixteen, Thomas left school and started to work for an architect. The architect drew designs of new buildings and planned ways to repair old ones.

In 1862, Thomas moved to London and he became an assistant to a famous architect. Thomas enjoyed living in London. He visited theatres and art galleries, and he read lots of books. Soon he began to write poetry, although none of his poems were published at this time.

In 1867, Thomas decided to return to Dorchester. In the town, he worked as an architect's assistant. But now he knew that he wanted to be a writer. He wrote a novel, but no one wanted to publish it. This did not stop Thomas writing, and soon he was working on a second novel.

In 1870, the architect sent Thomas to the county of Cornwall, in the far west of England. His job was to make drawings of the church in the village of St Juliot. He also had to find out if the church could be repaired or rebuilt.

This visit to Cornwall changed Thomas's life completely because he fell in love with Emma Lavinia Gifford. Emma had fair hair and blue eyes and she liked poetry and novels. She also wanted to be a writer.

Emma encouraged Thomas to write more novels, and in 1871, one of these novels – *Desperate Remedies* – was published. Thomas did not earn much money from the book. However, his next novel, *Under the Greenwood Tree* (1872), was more successful. It is a story about the working people of Dorset at the time of Thomas's own father and grandfather.

Far From the Madding Crowd was published in 1874. It is one of Hardy's greatest novels. The title comes from the words in a poem. Hardy writes about people who live in quiet, beautiful places that are far away from noisy, busy towns. But these people's lives are full of sadness and pain and madness.

Thomas and Emma got married and went to live in Dorchester. In the twenty years that followed, Thomas wrote more successful novels and short stories. His stories were set in a part of England which Hardy called Wessex. Wessex included the counties of Devon, Berkshire, Dorset, Wiltshire, Somerset and Hampshire. (See the map on page 3.)

Hardy's best-known novels are: *The Return of the Native* (1878), *The Trumpet-Major* (1880), *The Mayor of Casterbridge* (1886), *The Woodlanders* (1887), *Tess of the d'Urbervilles* (1891) and *Jude the Obscure* (1896).

After 1895, when he finished *Jude the Obscure*, Thomas Hardy wrote no more novels. *Jude the Obscure* is a very unhappy story. It shows arguments[2] between working people and well-educated people. And the story tells about sexual relationships between people who are not married. Many readers were shocked by this book and suddenly Hardy was no longer a popular writer. For the last thirty years of his life, he wrote only poetry. Many books of his poems were published during this time.

The last years of Thomas and Emma's marriage were not happy. Thomas did not speak to Emma and he did not care when she was ill. But when she died in 1912, Thomas felt guilty[3] and unhappy. Suddenly he wrote many poems about Emma and about the early days of their relationship. In 1914, Hardy married again. His new wife, Florence Dugdale, was much younger than Thomas. But Thomas could not forget his first wife. He made Florence very unhappy because he thought about Emma all the time.

Thomas Hardy died on 11th January, 1928. His body was buried[4] in Westminster Abbey, the famous church in London. But Hardy's heart was buried with Emma, in a churchyard in Dorset.

A Note About This Story

Most of Thomas Hardy's stories are about the people who worked on the farms and in the small villages in the country area[5] which he called Wessex. In the 1800s, many country people were poor and their lives were hard. They did things in the same way that their parents and grandparents had done them. They also did special things on special days of the year – these were their customs. One of their customs was to celebrate[6] spring – the time when trees and plants begin to grow again, and young animals are born.

In the nineteenth century, country people worked very hard every month of the year. They did not earn much money and farm work was dirty and difficult. Every member of a family had to work – even small children. Until 1886, country children did not go to school. They helped their mothers and fathers in the fields. After 1886, all children were able to go to school for a few years.

After their work was finished, farm workers often went to inns[7] and drank large amounts of alcohol. When they were drunk, they could forget about their troubles.

At this time, most country people walked, or travelled in vehicles pulled by horses. Railway lines were not yet built to all parts of the country.

Farm workers did many different jobs. In the spring, they planted the cereal crops[8] or vegetable crops in the fields. They repaired the farm buildings. They made and repaired the hedges[9] and walls which surrounded the fields.

At the end of the summer, the crops were harvested[10]. After a harvest, farmers took their crops to a corn exchange[11] and sold them.

Farm workers also took care of the animals – chickens, sheep, cows and horses. Dairy farmers kept cows and sold their milk. The men and women who took care of the herds of cows were called dairymen and dairymaids. Shepherds took care of the herds of sheep.

Most country people lived in cottages. These simple, small houses, and the large farms where people worked, belonged to rich landowners. On one day each week, there was a market in the larger villages or towns. At markets, people could buy or sell vegetables, animals and grain. They might also buy furniture, clothes or other things that they needed.

Each year, farmers hired[12] men, woman and children to work on their farms. They also hired servants to work in their homes. If they could not work, families had to leave their little cottages and find somewhere else to live. When people wanted to find work, they went to hiring fairs. These meetings were held in towns' markets in the month of February. The farm workers waited to be chosen by a farmer or landowner who wanted men or women to work on their land.

By the 1880s, machines were coming onto the farms to help the farm workers. But these machines were noisy and dangerous. Farm workers had to work faster and for more hours so that they could keep the machines running well.

1

Gabriel Oak

Farmer Gabriel Oak was a quiet, sensible man. He was twenty-eight years old and unmarried. And he was a man of good character[13]. On Sundays, he went to church and prayed. During the week, he worked in the fields of his farm.

On a sunny morning in December, Gabriel Oak walked across his field on Norcombe Hill, in the county of Wessex. He looked towards the road which went between Emminster and Chalk-Newton and saw a bright yellow wagon[14]. Two horses were pulling the heavy wagon slowly along the road. The driver was walking beside the wagon, which was loaded[15] with furniture. A woman was sitting on top of the furniture. She was young and very attractive.

Suddenly, the driver called to her. 'Something has fallen off the wagon, miss! I'll go back and get it.'

The young woman waited quietly. She did not get down from the wagon to help the driver. After several minutes, she looked back to see if the wagon driver was returning. He was not, so she opened a small package that was beside her. She took a mirror from the package and held it up to her face. As she looked in the mirror, she smiled.

The sun shone down on to the woman's red jacket, her pretty face and her dark hair. Gabriel Oak watched her and smiled. The girl did not touch her hat, or her hair. She simply looked at herself and smiled. Then she heard the wagon driver returning to the wagon. She put the mirror into the package and waited for him to drive the horses forward.

When the wagon moved on, Gabriel Oak followed it to the tollgate[16]. As he came nearer to the wagon, Oak heard the driver arguing with the man at the gate.

'The toll is two pence,' said the gatekeeper. 'But this wagon is large. You must pay two pence extra.'

But the young woman would not pay the extra money.

Oak thought that two pence was too small an amount to argue about. He held out two pennies to the gatekeeper.

'Take this and let the young woman go through,' he said.

The young woman looked down at Oak. She did not thank him, but she told her driver to go on. Oak and the gatekeeper watched her as the wagon passed.

'She's a handsome woman,' said the gatekeeper.

'That's true,' said Oak. 'But unfortunately, she knows it.'

It was nearly midnight on 21st December, the shortest day of the year. There were no clouds in the dark sky and the stars were shining brightly. A cold wind was blowing, but it was not the sound of the wind that travellers could hear on Norcombe Hill. It was the sound of music. The music came from a little wooden shepherd's hut that belonged to Gabriel Oak. Inside the hut, Gabriel was playing a happy tune on his flute[17]. The hut was on wheels and it gave shelter for the shepherd in the winter and early spring. He stayed in the hut while he cared for his sheep. At this time of the year, the sheep were giving birth[18] to their lambs. It was warm and comfortable inside the hut. Oak had a small stove[19] to keep him warm. And he had some bread, cheese and beer[20].

Oak's father had been a shepherd and he had taught Gabriel all that he knew about sheep. Now the young man had two hundred sheep, two sheepdogs[21], and a farm of his own. He had not yet paid for the sheep, and it was important to guard the sheep and their young lambs during the night.

After a few minutes, Oak stopped playing his flute, picked up a lamp, and went outside. As he moved around the field, he held the light high and looked at each sheep. Twenty minutes later, he returned to the hut with a new-born lamb.

It was weak and cold. After an hour in the warm hut, the lamb became stronger. Oak took the little lamb back outside and left it with its mother.

Suddenly, he saw a light shining in a field next to his own farm. Lamplight was coming from a cowshed[22] that was built into the side of the hill. Oak walked down the hill until he stood above the roof of the wooden building. He looked through a hole in the roof.

Inside the cowshed, two women were sitting beside a cow and its young calf. A lamp was standing on the floor of the cowshed. The soft yellow light shone on the women and the animals. One woman was about fifty years old. The other was younger, but she was wearing a cloak[23] which hid her face.

'We can go home now,' said the older woman. 'I hope that the cows will be all right.'

'If we were rich, we could pay a man to do these things,' said the younger woman.

'Well we aren't rich, so we must do the work ourselves,' said the older woman. 'And you must help me, if you stay on the farm.'

'Aunt, I've lost my hat,' said the younger woman. 'The wind blew it into the next field.'

Suddenly the cloak fell back from the young woman's head and Oak saw her long black hair and her red jacket. Oak recognized[24] her at once. It was the young woman who had been in the yellow wagon. The young woman who liked to look at herself in the mirror. The young woman who owed him two pence.

The two women put the calf next to its mother. Then they picked up their lamp and went out of the hut and down the hill. Oak went back to his sheep.

When it began to get light, Oak remembered the girl's lost hat. He went to look for it in his field. He found the hat under a hedge and took it back to his hut.

Later in the morning, Oak saw the young woman on the road. He was surprised. She was riding her horse like a man. She did not ride sidesaddle[25], like a lady. She had pulled up her long skirt and each of her legs were down the sides of the horse. He smiled and watched her ride away down the hill.

An hour later, the young woman returned. She was riding sidesaddle now. Oak got the hat from his hut and stepped onto the road in front of her.

'I found a hat, miss,' he said. And he held it up towards her.

'It's mine,' she said. She smiled and took the hat. 'It flew off my head in the wind last night.'

'At one o'clock this morning?'

'Yes, how did you know that?' she asked.

'I was here, with my sheep.'

'You're Farmer Oak,' she said.

'Yes,' he said. 'And I saw you again, about an hour ago.'

Her face became red. She was remembering her ride down the hill. He had seen her riding astride, like a man! Oak turned away. He had not wanted to embarrass[26] her.

When he turned back, she was gone.

Five mornings and evenings went by. The young woman came to the cowshed to take care of the cows which had new-born calves. But she did not speak to Oak. He watched her each day, and his heart ached[27].

Then one evening he was very tired. He came back to his shepherd's hut and shut the door. It was a cold night and he was pleased to be near the warm stove. But he forgot to open one of the little windows. It was important to do this when a fire was burning in the stove and the door was shut. In a few minutes, Oak fell asleep.

When Oak opened his eyes again, his head was aching. He looked up and saw the face of the young woman. His head was in her arms and she was opening the top of his shirt.

'What's the matter?' asked Oak.

'Nothing now,' she replied. 'But you could have died. You forgot to open a window.'

'Oh,' said Oak. He wanted to stay with his head in her arms forever, but she made him sit up.

'I heard your dog barking[28],' she told him. 'It was trying to open the door of the hut. I came to see what was wrong.'

'You saved my life, miss,' said Oak. 'But – but I don't know your name. I know your aunt's name. It's Mrs Hurst. But I don't know yours.'

'You don't have to know my name,' she replied. 'And I don't like it.'

'You'll soon get a new name, when you marry.'

'Well, Farmer Oak!' she said. 'Do you always speak so – so – plainly?'

'I'm sorry, miss,' said Oak. 'I did not mean to be rude. I'm not clever with words. I'm a plain man and I speak plainly and honestly. But I do thank you. Please, let me shake your hand.'

Oak held the young woman's hand in his own. 'How soft it is,' he said quietly.

'You're thinking, "I would like to kiss her hand",' she said. 'Well, you can if you want to.'

'I wasn't thinking that at all, but —'

'Then you won't!' she said. And she pulled her hand away. 'Now you must find out my name,' she said, laughing. And she went away.

2

Bathsheba

Oak learnt that the young woman's name was Bathsheba Everdene. And he realized that he was in love. He thought about her all the time. He thought about her face, her hair, her soft hands. He said her name – 'Bathsheba!' – again and again.

'I must marry her!' he said to himself. 'She must be my wife, or I'll not be good for anything again!'

When Bathsheba no longer visited the cowshed, he went to her aunt's house. He knocked at the door of the farmhouse and Mrs Hurst opened the door.

'Mr Oak!' she said.

'Can I see Miss Everdene?' said Oak. 'I've brought a lamb

for her to care for. Its mother died. Girls sometimes like to take care of a lamb.'

'Well, I don't know,' said Mrs Hurst. 'Bathsheba is only a visitor here. She won't be staying long on my farm. And she's not here at the moment. Do you want to wait for her?'

'Yes, I'll wait,' said Oak and he sat in a chair. 'The lamb isn't the real reason I came here, Mrs Hurst. I want to ask Miss Everdene if she would like to be married. I would be very happy to marry her. Do you know if there are any other young men who want to marry her?'

'Oh, yes!' said Mrs Hurst. 'It's not surprising, because she's so pretty and so clever. The young men never come here, of course. But there are ten or more young men who want to marry her.'

'Oh, then I won't wait,' said Oak. 'I'm only an ordinary man. My best chance[29] was to be the first man to propose[30] to her.'

He was walking back across the fields, when he heard someone give a shout. He turned round and saw Bathsheba running after him.

'Farmer Oak!' she called. She stopped in front of him, breathing fast. 'My aunt made a mistake,' she said. 'There aren't any other young men who have proposed to me.'

'Is this true?' said Oak. 'I'm *very* happy to hear that!'

He held out his hand, but she quickly put her own hand behind her back.

'I have a nice little farmhouse and some good fields,' he went on. 'I haven't paid for the farm yet. But when we're married —'

'Farmer Oak,' Bathsheba said, surprised. 'I never said that I was going to marry you. I only wanted to tell you of my aunt's mistake.'

Oak was disappointed. 'Think about my proposal,' he said

softly. 'I'll wait, Miss Everdene. Please, Bathsheba. I love you more than my life!'

'I'll think about what you have said,' she replied. 'Give me time before I must answer.'

'I can make you happy,' he said. 'In a year or two, I will have earned more money. You can have a piano, and a little carriage which you can drive to the market each week.'

'I should like that,' she said.

'We'll be comfortable and happy in our home. And I'll be there, by the fire, whenever you look up. And whenever *I* look up, there *you* will be ...'

Bathsheba was silent for a few minutes, and he watched her.

Then she said, 'No, I don't want to marry you, Farmer Oak. A wedding in a church would be nice, and people would say nice things about me. But a husband —'

'Yes?' said Oak quickly.

'A husband would always *be there*,' she said. 'If I could have a wedding without having a husband . . . but I can't. So I won't marry anyone, not yet.'

'What a stupid thing to say!' said Oak. 'But my dear, why won't you marry me?'

'Because I don't love you,' she answered.

'But *I* love *you*,' said Oak. 'And I will love you and want you, until I die!'

'No, I'm sorry, Mr Oak,' she said. 'We couldn't be happy as man and wife. I'm too independent[31]. I need a husband who is a stronger character than me. And I live with my aunt and have no money. You need a woman with money. You need a rich wife who can buy more sheep for your farm and help it to grow.'

'But —' began Oak.

'No – no, I can't marry you,' said Bathsheba. Then she laughed. 'I don't love you. I would be stupid if I married you.'

Oak did not like people laughing at him. 'Then I'll not ask you again,' he said quietly.

It is not easy to stop loving someone. And Oak soon found out that this was true.

A few days after Oak's proposal, Bathsheba went to Weatherbury – which was more than twenty miles away. Had she gone to live in the town, or was she only visiting it? Oak did not know. But his love for Bathsheba grew stronger now that she was further away from him. And then something happened that changed his life.

One night, Oak came back to his house and called his two sheepdogs. But only the older dog came home. Oak did not worry about the younger dog.

'He'll come back soon,' he thought. And he went to bed.

Very early the next morning, as the sky began to get light, Oak woke up suddenly. He had heard the sound of sheep's bells[32] ringing. The sheep were running on the hill and the bells around their necks were ringing loudly. Oak knew that something was wrong. He jumped from his bed and put on his clothes quickly. Then he ran out of the house, down the lane, and onto Norcombe Hill.

Oak had two hundred and fifty sheep. Fifty sheep and their young lambs were in one field. Two hundred pregnant sheep were in a second field. Their lambs were going to be born in a week or two. And these sheep had disappeared.

Oak began to call the sheep. Then he saw that the fence was broken. He ran through the hole in the fence and looked up to the top of the hill. His younger dog was standing there. Suddenly, Oak knew the terrible truth. The young dog had become excited and had chased[33] the sheep.

Oak ran to the top of the hill and looked down. Below the other side of the hill, there was a deep chalk pit[34].

At the bottom of the pit lay his sheep – two hundred of

them. And inside the dead or dying bodies of the sheep, were two hundred unborn lambs.

At first, Oak felt very sorry for the sheep and their lambs. But moments later, he realized that he had lost more than his sheep.

'I'm ruined[35]!' he thought. 'The sheep were not insured[36], and I have no more money. I cannot buy more sheep.'

The next day, Oak took his gun and shot the young dog.

A bank had given him money so that could buy the sheep. Now he had to sell everything so that he could repay the debt[37].

'Thank God that I'm not married to Bathsheba,' he thought. 'I've lost everything. I have nothing but the clothes that I'm wearing.'

3

The Fire

Two months later, Gabriel Oak was at the market in the town of Casterbridge. It was now the month of February.

Oak was at the hiring fair. He wanted to work as a farm manager [38]. But he had been unlucky. No one had hired him. During the morning, he saw a regiment[39] of soldiers leaving the town.

'Should I become a soldier?' Gabriel thought. 'The army would pay me each month. It would give me food, clothes and somewhere to live.'

The next day, Gabriel decided to go to another village which was ten miles on the other side of Weatherbury. He would try to find work there. Perhaps someone would hire him as a shepherd. Gabriel bought a shepherd's crook[40] and then he started walking.

'Is Bathsheba still living in Weatherbury?' he thought.

After he had walked three or four miles, Gabriel saw a wagon standing beneath some trees. There was no horse with the wagon, but there was a large pile of hay[41] on the top of it.

'I'm tired and that hay will make a good, soft bed,' Gabriel thought. He climbed into the wagon and covered himself with hay. He was asleep after only a few minutes.

When Gabriel woke up again, it was dark and the wagon was moving. He could hear men's voices.

'She's not married and she's a very handsome woman,' said one man. 'But she knows that she's pretty.'

The other man gave a short laugh. 'I'm much too shy[42] to look at her,' he said. 'Tell me, Billy Smallbury, does she pay her workers well?'

'I don't know, Joe Poorgrass.'

'Are these men talking about Bathsheba?' thought Gabriel. 'No. The woman they're speaking about is the owner of a farm.'

Gabriel looked at the road they were travelling on. He guessed[43] that the wagon was near Weatherbury now. He jumped down onto the road and climbed over a gate into a field. The two men in the wagon did not see him.

Gabriel had to find a place to sleep for the rest of the night. He began walking. After a few minutes, he saw a strange light about half a mile away. Gabriel watched the light growing bigger and brighter. Something was burning!

Gabriel ran towards the fire and saw that a rick of straw[44] was burning. The powerful flames were reaching across to another rick – a rick of wheat. And past this, there were more wheat-ricks. All the wheat from the farm's fields was kept in these ricks and soon they would be burnt.

Farm workers were running around the farmyard[45]. People were shouting, 'Fire, fire!' But nobody seemed to know what to do. Nobody knew how to put out the flames.

'Quickly! Get a rick-cloth[46]!' shouted Gabriel. 'Make it wet and hang it between the straw-rick and the wheat-rick. The cloth might stop the flames reaching across to the other ricks!'

Some of the men did this. They found a rick-cloth and put it into a pond to make it wet. Then they pulled the wet cloth up onto two tall poles between the ricks.

'Get a ladder!' shouted Gabriel. 'And some buckets of water. Hurry!'

'The ladder that was against the straw-rick was burnt,' shouted a man.

Gabriel quickly climbed to the top of the wheat-rick. He used his hands and feet to pull himself up. Gabriel began to beat the flames which were on the stalks of wheat with his shepherd's crook. He was trying to put out the flames.

Billy Smallbury – one of the men who had been driving the wagon – had found another ladder. He put it against the wheat-rick and climbed up onto the rick with a bucket of water. He poured the water over Oak's face and clothes to stop the flames burning him.

On the ground, groups of farm workers tried to stop the fire, but they could not do very much.

A dark-haired young woman sat on a horse, away from the heat and smoke. She watched the workers moving around the ricks. Another young woman, one of her maids, stood next to her.

'Who's that man on the rick, Maryann?' asked the young woman.

'He's a shepherd, I think, ma'am[47],' said the maid.

'Who does he work for?' asked the woman on the horse.

'I don't know, ma'am,' replied Maryann. 'Nobody knows. I've asked many people. He's a stranger.'

The young woman on the horse called to one of the men.

'Jan Coggan! Are the wheat-ricks safe?'

'They're safe now, ma'am,' replied Coggan. 'Thanks to the shepherd.'

'Maryann, go and thank the shepherd for me,' said the woman on the horse.

After about ten minutes, Gabriel Oak climbed down to the ground and Maryann went across to him.

'The farmer wants to thank you,' she told Oak.

'Where is he?' asked Oak. Perhaps there was work for a shepherd here.

'It's not a "he", it's a "she",' said Maryann.

'A woman farmer?'

'Yes, and a rich one, too!' said a villager who was near them. 'Her uncle died a few months ago, and now this farm is hers. She has business in every bank in Casterbridge.'

Oak walked across to the woman on the horse. The flames had burned small holes in his clothes. His face was dirty from the smoke. He took off his hat, and spoke politely.

'Do you want a shepherd, miss?' he asked.

And then he saw the young woman's face more clearly. It was Bathsheba Everdene.

She did not reply, so Oak asked the question again. This time there was sadness in his voice. 'Do you want a shepherd, miss?'

Bathsheba Everdene had almost forgotten Oak's proposal of marriage. But she remembered it now – two months later. She felt a little sorry for Gabriel. But she was pleased for herself. She saw that Gabriel was now a poor man and she had been luckier.

'Yes,' she said, kindly. 'I do want to hire a shepherd.'

'He's the right man, ma'am,' said one of the farm workers.

'Yes, he is!' said a second man.

'Speak to my farm manager, Mr Pennyways,' Bathsheba

said to Gabriel. Then she turned her horse and rode away.

Gabriel spoke to Mr Pennyways about his new work as a shepherd. Then he followed the farm workers towards the village. He needed to find a place to live. As he walked, Gabriel thought about Bathsheba. She was not the young girl that he remembered. She was a farm owner now.

Gabriel reached an old tree. Beside the tree, there was a churchyard which was surrounded by old trees. Suddenly he saw a young woman standing beneath one of the trees.

'Is this the right way to the village?' he asked her.

'Yes,' she replied with a sweet, low voice. 'Are you a stranger in Weatherbury?'

'Yes,' said Gabriel. 'I'm the new shepherd. I've just arrived.'

'You're only a shepherd? Oh, I thought that you were a farmer.' She spoke quietly and sadly. 'Please don't tell anyone in the village that you've seen me. I don't want them to know about me.'

Gabriel felt sorry for the sad young woman. He gave her a little money before he went on.

4

A Valentine

Gabriel Oak went to an inn called Warren's Malthouse. There, he found other farm workers drinking beer.

'Come in shepherd!' said one of the men, when he saw Gabriel at the door. 'You're welcome in Weatherbury, although we don't know your name.'

'My name is Gabriel Oak,' he told them, and sat down.

'Tell me, is Miss Everdene a good employer?'

'We don't know,' said Jan Coggan. 'She came here a few days ago, after her uncle died. She owns his farm now, and she's going to keep it.'

'I need somewhere to stay,' said Gabriel. 'Does anyone have a room in a cottage that I can pay for?'

Jan Coggan told Gabriel that he could stay in his home, and the two men left the inn together.

Another farm worker – Henery Fray – also went out of the inn at the same time. But he returned minutes later, looking very excited.

'I've just heard some news about Pennyways,' he said. 'Miss Everdene caught him stealing wheat. She's sent him away!'

Everyone began to talk about Pennyways – Miss Everdene's dishonest farm manager. Henery Fray bought another mug of beer. But before he had lifted the mug to his mouth, another farm worker came running into the inn.

'Have you heard the news?' he asked.

'Is this news about Pennyways?' said Henery. 'Or is it *more* news, Laban Tall?'

'It's news about Fanny Robin – Miss Everdene's youngest maid,' said Laban. 'Fanny has disappeared! Miss Everdene wants to speak to all of us before we go to bed.'

All the workers went along the lane to Weatherbury Farm, where Bathsheba lived. When she saw them arrive, she opened a window and called down to them.

'Tomorrow morning, I want two or three of you to look for Fanny Robin,' she said. 'Was she courting[48] any young man in the village?'

From another open window, Maryann spoke. 'She wasn't courting anyone in the village, ma'am,' said the maid. 'But she's been visiting Casterbridge. She's been courting a soldier at the barracks[49] there, but I don't know his name.'

'Billy Smallbury,' said Bathsheba, looking down at a heavy young man who was carrying a lamp. 'If Fanny doesn't return tomorrow, you must go to Casterbridge. Try to find out the soldier's name.'

Then she closed her window and the men went home.

The next day, Bathsheba and her maid, Liddy Smallbury, were looking through some books and papers that had belonged to Bathsheba's uncle. Suddenly there was a knock at the front door. Liddy went to the window and looked out.

'It's Mr Boldwood, ma'am,' she said.

Bathsheba looked at the dust on her dress and hands. 'I can't see him now,' she said. 'Go and ask him what he wants.'

Liddy came back a few minutes later. 'Mr Boldwood asked about Fanny,' she said. 'He worries about her. Fanny had no friends or family when she was a young girl, and Mr Boldwood paid for her to go to school. He's a very kind man.'

'Who is he?' asked Bathsheba.

'He's your neighbour,' said Liddy. 'He owns Little Weatherbury, the farm beside yours. He's about forty years old and very rich. All the girls of the village have tried to marry Mr Boldwood, but he's just not interested.'

Later that day, Bathsheba sent for all her farm workers. They met together in one of the large farm buildings.

'As you know, Pennyways has left the farm,' she told them. 'But I'm not going to hire another farm manager. I'm going to manage the farm myself.'

The men looked at each other. They were very surprised. Did this young woman know how to manage a farm? But before they could speak, Bathsheba turned to Billy Smallbury.

'Billy, what have you learnt about Fanny Robin and her soldier?' she asked.

'Many of the soldiers left Casterbridge last week,' said Billy. 'I think that Fanny's young man is a member of the

Eleventh Dragoon Guards. He went to Melchester with the rest of his regiment. Fanny has followed him. But nobody knows his name.'

That night, many miles north of Weatherbury, a person dressed in a cloak moved along a path between a river and a high stone building. Grey clouds were low in the sky and it was very cold. Snow was falling. The bell of Melchester's church clock rang ten times as the person walked slowly towards the army barracks' building.

A few moments later, the person stopped and threw a stone up at a high window.

The window opened. 'Who's there?' called a man's voice.

'Sergeant Troy?' a girl's voice asked. 'Sergeant Frank Troy?

'Yes,' replied the man, leaning out of the window. He wore a red coat and blue trousers – the uniform of a dragoon guardsman. The dragoon looked down at the girl standing below him. Snow fell on to her face and cloak.

'Frank? This is Fanny Robin!'

'Fanny! How did you find me?' asked Troy.

'I asked someone which was the window of your room,' she said. 'Frank, are you pleased to see me?'

'Oh – well, yes.'

'When will we be married, Frank? You promised —'

'Wait!' he said. 'I didn't expect[50] you to come here so soon. I didn't expect you to come *at all*.'

Fanny began to cry. 'Frank, I love you! And you said lots of times that you would marry me.'

'Don't cry,' he said. 'I will marry you, if I made that promise. I'll come and see you tomorrow.'

'I'm staying in rooms at Mrs Twill's house in North Street,' said Fanny. 'Goodnight, Frank – goodnight!'

The next time that there was a market in Casterbridge, Bathsheba went into the town. She went to the Corn Exchange. She was the only woman there, and all the men stared at her. All except one – Farmer William Boldwood of Little Weatherbury Farm. This rich, handsome gentleman did not seem to notice[51] her. Bathsheba was surprised and annoyed[52]. She was a beautiful woman and she knew this. Most men found her attractive[53].

One Sunday, Bathsheba was talking with Liddy. It was the thirteenth of February and a dark, cold winter afternoon. The two women were sitting together by the fire, in the kitchen of the farmhouse.

'Did you see Mr Boldwood in church this morning, ma'am?' asked Liddy.

'No,' said Bathsheba.

'He was sitting opposite you. Are you *sure* that you didn't see him?' said Liddy, smiling.

'I did not!' replied Bathsheba

'And he didn't seem to notice you,' said Liddy.

'Why should he?' said Bathsheba.

'Every other man in the church looked at you,' said Liddy. 'But Mr Boldwood didn't even turn his head towards you.'

Bathsheba was silent for some minutes. Then she said, 'Oh, I bought a valentine card[54] yesterday. I almost forgot about it.'

'A valentine card!' said Liddy, excitedly. 'Who is it for? Farmer Boldwood?'

'No!' said Bathsheba. 'It's for Teddy Coggan, Jan Coggan's son.' She took the card from her desk. 'Teddy is a lovely child. I wanted him to get his first valentine card from me.'

'It would be fun to send the card to Boldwood!' said Liddy, laughing.

Bathsheba thought about this for a moment. All the other

important men in the area admired her, but Boldwood did not even notice her. She was annoyed.

'You're right, Liddy,' she said. 'We'll send the card to Boldwood! It will be a good joke.'

Bathsheba wrote Boldwood's name and address on the front of an envelope, and put the card inside it. Then she laughed and wrote the words: MARRY ME on the back of the envelope.

That evening, the valentine was sent to Boldwood. It was a joke – but Bathsheba would soon wish that she had never done it.

On the evening of St Valentine's Day – the fourteenth of February – Farmer Boldwood sat down to eat his supper. On the dining table next to him, was the valentine card.

Since it had arrived that morning, Boldwood had asked himself these questions many times. 'Who has sent the card? MARRY ME are the words on the back of the envelope. Which woman would send such a message to me?'

Boldwood could not sleep that night. At dawn, he got out of his bed. But he did not eat breakfast. He went out into the fields and watched the sun come up over the cold, snowy hills. Then he walked back to the road.

Suddenly he heard a noise behind him and turned around. The mail-cart[55] was coming along the road towards his farmhouse. When he reached Boldwood, the driver stopped and held out a letter towards him.

The farmer took the envelope and started to open it.

But the mail-cart driver said, 'I don't think that the letter is for you, sir. I think it's for your shepherd.'

Boldwood looked at the envelope and read the words: *To the New Shepherd, Weatherbury Farm, Near Casterbridge*.

'You've made a mistake,' said Boldwood. 'This letter isn't for me, or my shepherd. It's for Miss Everdene's shepherd –

Gabriel Oak – at Weatherbury Farm. This is *Little* Weatherbury Farm.'

At that moment, he saw someone moving on the hill. 'There's Oak. I'll take the letter to him myself.'

When he reached the top of the hill, Farmer Boldwood called to the shepherd. 'Oak! I met the mail-cart, and this letter was delivered to me. But it was a mistake, the letter is for you. I'm sorry that I started to open it.'

Gabriel Oak took the letter from the envelope and read it.

Dear Friend

I do not know your name, but I want to thank you. You were kind to me on the night that I left Weatherbury. I am going to be married to the young man who has been courting me. His name is Sergeant Troy and he is a man of honour[56]*. He would not want me to keep your money, so I am returning it to you.*

Please do not tell anyone about this letter. As soon as we are husband and wife, we will come to Weatherbury.

Thank you again for your kindness.

Fanny Robin

Gabriel gave the letter to Boldwood. 'I know that you're worried about Fanny Robin,' he said. 'You must read this.'

Boldwood read the letter and looked unhappy.

'What kind of man is Sergeant Troy?' asked Gabriel. 'Is he a good and honest man?'

'He's young and handsome,' said Boldwood. 'And many women love him. But I don't think that Troy wants to marry anyone. Poor Fanny!'

After a moment, Boldwood put his hand in his pocket. He took out the envelope containing the valentine card.

'Tell me, Oak,' he said. 'Do you know who wrote this?'

Gabriel looked at the writing on the envelope. 'It's Miss Everdene's handwriting,' he said. He looked quickly at Boldwood.

The farmer turned his head and looked across the hill.

'A person who receives a valentine will try and find out who sent it,' he said. 'Everyone expects that will happen.' But Boldwood spoke seriously. He was not enjoying the joke.

A few minutes later, he returned to his house.

A day or two later, a handsome young dragoon walked into All Souls' church. He was wearing his red jacket and blue trousers and carried a shining helmet with a tall crest[57]. A long sword hung from a belt at the sergeant's waist.

The dragoon waited for the young woman who was to be his wife. He waited and waited, but she did not come. The silver spurs[58] on the dragoon's boots rang like little bells as he walked up and down. After half an hour, he left the church.

As he walked away from the church, he met a young woman. She was running towards the church. When she saw the soldier, the young woman looked frightened.

'Oh, Frank!' she cried. 'I made a mistake. I went to the wrong church! I went to All Saints' church! I'm sorry! But it doesn't matter, we can be married tomorrow instead.'

'You fool, Fanny!' said Sergeant Francis Troy. 'Get married tomorrow? No! I waited at the church, but you didn't come. You embarrassed me. I won't do this again for a long time, I promise you!'

5

Mr Boldwood's Proposal

On Saturday morning, Farmer William Boldwood was at Casterbridge market when Bathsheba arrived.

For several nights, Boldwood's dreams had been about Bathsheba Everdene. But now, for the first time, he looked at her closely. He saw her black hair, the shape of her face, her clothes. And he saw that she was beautiful.

'*This* is the woman who has asked me to marry her!' he thought.

Bathsheba saw him watching her, and smiled.

'He knows who sent the valentine card,' she thought. 'But only a joke made him notice me.'

Suddenly, Bathsheba was sorry. She respected[59] Boldwood. She was sorry that she had disturbed[60] this quiet, calm man's life.

Boldwood was a serious man, but he had strong feelings. As the weeks passed and spring came, he watched Bathsheba. He watched her from his fields next to her farm. At last he decided to speak to her.

One morning in May, Boldwood saw Bathsheba at the

sheep-washing pool[61] with Gabriel Oak and her other farm workers. She was watching the men push each sheep down into the water. The women were watching and laughing as the water splashed over everyone. When she saw Boldwood, Bathsheba moved away and began to walk towards the river. Boldwood followed her.

'Miss Everdene!' he said, when they were both walking next to the river. 'I can't think sensibly about anything or anybody since I saw you clearly. So I've come to make you a proposal of marriage. More than anything in the world, I want you to be my wife.'

Bathsheba tried to stay calm. She stopped walking and looked at him. 'Mr Boldwood,' she said carefully. 'I admire[62] you and respect you, but I can't marry you.'

'Miss Everdene, my life is empty without you!' said Boldwood. 'Oh, I wish that I could court you with pretty words! Let me say again and again that I love you! I want you to be my wife. I'm speaking to you now because you gave me hope. You wrote "Marry Me" on the valentine.'

'I was wrong and foolish to send you that valentine,' said Bathsheba. 'Please forgive me! I promise that I'll never play jokes again.'

'No, no! Don't say this!' cried Boldwood. His eyes shone fiercely[63] as he spoke and he stood close to her.

'I don't love you, Mr Boldwood,' said Bathsheba. She was frightened by his strong feelings. 'Please, don't speak about this anymore. I can't think clearly. I didn't know that you were going to say this to me.'

'Don't say that you'll never love me!' he said quickly. 'Let me speak to you about this again. Let me hope that one day you will accept my proposal!'

'No, don't hope!' Bathsheba replied. 'Give me time. Let me think.'

'Yes, I'll give you time,' he said, quietly. 'I'll wait.'

Bathsheba was not in love with Boldwood, so she was able to think calmly about his proposal. Many women would be proud to marry Boldwood. She knew this. The farmer was a man of good character, and he was rich.

'I started a foolish game by sending that valentine,' she thought. 'But perhaps I should be honest now. Perhaps I *should* marry him. But I can't do it.'

The day after Boldwood made his proposal, Bathsheba went to see Gabriel Oak.

'Tell me,' she said to him. 'Did the workers say anything about me and Mr Boldwood?'

'They think that you will probably marry him before the end of the year,' said Gabriel.

'How stupid!' said Bathsheba. 'I want you to tell them that it's not true.'

Gabriel was surprised when he heard this. But he was also happy. 'Yes, I can tell them,' he said. 'But do you want *my* opinion[64], Bathsheba?'

'You should call me Miss Everdene,' she said, coldly. But she *did* want Gabriel's opinion. She respected him more than anyone else. 'Well, what do you have to say?' she asked.

'You were wrong to send Farmer Boldwood the valentine card,' said Gabriel. 'It was unkind and dishonest.'

Bathsheba's face became red and she said angrily, 'I'm not interested in your opinion! And why am I unkind and dishonest? Is it because I didn't marry *you*?'

'No,' said Gabriel quietly. 'I stopped thinking about my proposal a long time ago.'

'And you'll never wish to ask again, I suppose?' she said. But she expected him to say that he still loved her.

'No, I don't wish to,' he said. 'But I repeat. You were wrong when you sent Mr Boldwood that valentine. It was cruel and dishonest.'

'I won't let you to speak to me like that!' said Bathsheba. She was shaking with anger. 'Please leave my farm at the end of the week!'

'I'll be happier if I go now,' said Gabriel.

'Very well, go!' she said. 'I don't want to see you again.'

Twenty-four hours later, three of Bathsheba's farm workers came running to her house with terrible news.

'Sixty of your sheep broke the fence around their field!' said Joe Poorgrass.

'And they got into a field of clover[65]!' said Henery Fray.

'They've eaten the clover and they're all sick,' said Laban Tall. 'Their stomachs[66] are swollen[67]! They'll die if someone doesn't help them!'

Bathsheba hurried out to the field with the men. Her sheep were lying on the ground. Their stomachs were very swollen and they groaned in pain.

'Oh, what can we do?' she cried.

'Someone must make a hole in their sides and let out the air,' said Laban. 'You need a special tool to make a small hole.'

'And there's only one man who *can* do this,' said Joseph Poorgrass. 'Gabriel Oak.'

'Don't speak his name!' said Bathsheba, angrily. 'I don't want to hear it. Perhaps Farmer Boldwood will help us.'

'No, ma'am,' said Laban. 'This happened to two of *his* sheep a few days ago. He sent for Shepherd Oak, and Shepherd Oak saved them.'

'I'll never send for him – never!' said Bathsheba.

Suddenly, one of the sheep jumped up, then fell heavily onto the ground. It did not move and Bathsheba went to look at it. The sheep was dead.

'Oh, what shall I do – what shall I do!' she cried. She looked at the dead sheep for several moments. Then she said, 'Laban, take a horse and ride quickly. Find Oak and give him this order. Tell the shepherd that he must return immediately.'

Laban took one of the horses from a field and rode away. Bathsheba watched the man and the horse disappear over the hill. Then she began to walk up and down beside the sick sheep. After an hour, Laban returned. He was alone.

'Well?' said Bathsheba. 'Where is Shepherd Oak?'

'Gabriel won't come until you ask him politely, ma'am,' said Laban.

'What! Is that his answer?'

Suddenly, another sheep jumped into the air and fell dead. Bathsheba began to cry. 'Oh, how can Oak be so cruel!'

'Gabriel is a good man, ma'am,' said Laban. 'He'll come if you *ask* him, and not *order* him.'

Bathsheba hurried back to the house. She wrote these words in a note: *Do not desert me*[68], *Gabriel.*

Laban rode away with the note. Fifteen minutes later, he

returned with Gabriel Oak. Gabriel went straight to the sheep and began to work on them. He pushed a sharp tool into the side of each sheep and let out the air in their swollen stomachs. He saved all except four of the animals.

Bathsheba came and stood beside him.

'Gabriel, I – I was wrong to send you away. Will you stay with me?' she asked, smiling.

'I will,' he said.

6

Sergeant Troy

It was the first day of June. At this time in the summer, the sheep were sheared. In the great barn, the men cut the wool off the sheep and the women prepared the wool to sell it at the market. Bathsheba went to the barn to watch them working. She watched Gabriel Oak bending over a sheep and cutting the wool from its body. At last, he stood up straight and wiped the sweat from his face. The sheep ran out of the barn. Its slim, white body shone in the bright sunshine.

'Twenty-three minutes!' Bathsheba said to Gabriel. 'I've never seen a sheep sheared in less than half an hour.'

Gabriel smiled. He was pleased that she had noticed him. Then he saw Farmer Boldwood at the barn door, and his happiness disappeared.

Bathsheba and Farmer Boldwood spoke quietly together, then Bathsheba went into the house. When she came out a few minutes later, she was wearing a green riding-habit[69].

Oak watched Boldwood and Bathsheba get onto their horses and ride away.

That evening, there was a big supper for all the farm

workers. A long table had been put on the grass outside the house. The men, women and children had all worked hard and now they were going to enjoy a good meal and plenty of beer. Bathsheba sat at one end of the table, and she asked Gabriel to sit at the other end. At that moment, Farmer Boldwood arrived.

'I'm late,' he said to Bathsheba. 'I'm sorry.'

'Gabriel, will you move again?' said Bathsheba. 'Let Mr Boldwood sit there.'

Silently, Gabriel Oak moved to another seat.

After their supper, the farm workers sang songs and told stories. Gabriel played his flute as everyone sang.

William Boldwood usually wore dark grey clothes. But tonight he wore a bright new coat and a beautiful white silk waistcoat[70]. He seemed very happy, and so did Bathsheba. Gabriel watched them sitting together at the end of the table. Boldwood was usually a serious, silent man. Tonight, he was talking quietly to Bathsheba and smiling.

The sun went down and the sky became dark. Soon it was time for the workers to leave. Bathsheba said goodnight to everyone, then she and Boldwood went inside the house.

When Bathsheba and Boldwood were alone, the farmer got down onto his knees. 'Now, please tell me,' he said, kneeling in front of Bathsheba. 'Promise me that you'll marry me.'

'I'll try to love you,' said Bathsheba. 'And I'll marry you, if I believe that I can be a good wife to you. But I can't make a promise tonight. Please don't make me give you an answer. You're going away tomorrow for five or six weeks. When you come back, perhaps I'll be able to make you a promise. But remember, I'm not promising to be your wife now.'

'That is all right,' said Boldwood. 'I don't ask for more. Goodnight, Miss Everdene.'

That evening, Bathsheba took a lamp and walked around the farm. She checked that everything was safe for the night. As she was walking along the path back to the farmhouse, she heard footsteps. Someone was coming through the trees, towards her.

Bathsheba was standing on the darkest part of the path. When she and the stranger met, something caught the edge of her skirt and held it.

'Oh, have I hurt you?' said a man's voice.

'No,' said Bathsheba. And she pulled at her skirt.

'Give me your lamp,' said the man. 'I'll see what has happened.' And he bent down and shone the lamp at his feet.

Bathsheba saw that the stranger was a dragoon. He wore a bright red coat, and the sharp spur on one of his boots was caught in the bottom of her skirt. Bathsheba began to pull at her skirt again, but she could not get it free.

'You're a prisoner, miss,' said the soldier, smiling. 'I must cut your skirt if you want to get away quickly.'

'Yes, please do that,' she said.

He looked up at her. He was very handsome and his white teeth shone beneath his black moustache.

'Thank you for letting me see your beautiful face,' he said.

Bathsheba's face became hot and red. 'I didn't choose to show you my face! Please, hurry! I think that you're trying to keep me here!'

'Don't be angry,' said the young man. 'I've seen many women, but none as beautiful as you.'

'Who *are* you?'

'I'm not a stranger in Weatherbury,' he said. 'My name's Sergeant Troy. There! Now you're free. But I wish that you weren't. I wish that we were tied together forever, Beauty.'

Bathsheba pulled her skirt away from his boot and hurried along the path to her house. She did not look back at him.

Inside the farmhouse, Liddy was preparing to go to bed. Bathsheba asked her about the soldier. From Liddy, she learnt that Sergeant Francis Troy had been born in Weatherbury. He came from a good family and his father had been a doctor. Francis Troy had received a good education. But when he lost all his money, he had become a soldier. Troy was a sergeant in a regiment of dragoons. Everyone admired the dragoons – they rode tall horses and wore smart uniforms. And women especially liked handsome Sergeant Troy.

Bathsheba thought about the young soldier and smiled. She could not be angry with Troy for long. He had said that she was beautiful. He had called her Beauty.

'Boldwood has *never* said that I'm beautiful,' she thought.

A week or two later, Bathsheba walked down to her fields. She wanted to watch her farm workers cutting the hay. She was surprised to see Sergeant Troy helping them. It was a hot, bright day and Troy's coat was like a red flame. The dragoon was standing with the men who were pulling their sharp scythes[71] through the long grass. He saw her and came across the field to speak to her.

'Miss Everdene! I didn't realize that I was speaking to the "Queen of the Corn Exchange[72]" the other evening!' he said, laughing. 'I often helped your uncle in these fields when I was a boy. Today I've been helping you.'

'I suppose that I must thank you,' said Bathsheba.

'It's not necessary,' he replied.

'Good,' she said. 'Because I don't really want to thank you for anything.'

'Oh, I'm sorry. I made you angry the other evening,' he said. 'But I spoke honestly. I can't be the only person to tell you that you're beautiful. Don't others tell you this, too?'

'No – well – Liddy says that they do,' said Bathsheba.

'There! It's the truth!' said Troy. 'Now, please forgive me.'

'Well, perhaps you didn't mean to be rude to me the other evening,' said Bathsheba. 'Thank you for helping the men today. But please don't speak to me unless I speak to you.'

'Oh, Miss Everdene, that's too hard!' said Troy. '*You'll* never speak to me. And I'm going away again in a month.'

'Do you really care that I might not speak to you?' Bathsheba asked.

'Perhaps I'm foolish. But yes, I do care,' Troy replied. 'I loved you from the moment that I saw you the other night – and I love you now!'

'You can't love me! You don't!' said Bathsheba. 'I won't listen to you any more. What time is it? I've wasted too much time[73] here already.'

'Haven't you got a watch?' asked Troy. And before she could stop him, he put a heavy gold watch into her hand.

'Please take it,' he said softly. 'It belonged to my mother's family, who were noblemen. She gave it to my father and the watch became mine after he died.'

'But, Sergeant Troy, I can't take this! A gold watch!'

'Please keep it, Miss Everdene,' Troy said. 'I loved my father, but I love you more.'

He was not playing games with her now. He was serious. His eyes shone with love as he looked at her.

'How can you *love* me?' said Bathsheba. 'This is only the second time that you've spoken to me. Please, take back the watch. I can't have it.'

'Very well, I'll take it back,' he said. And she gave the watch to him. 'But will you speak to me for the few weeks that I'm here?' he asked.

'Yes – no – I don't know!' Bathsheba cried. 'Oh, why did you come?'

'Will you let me work in your fields?' Frank Troy asked.

'Yes, if it pleases you,' she said.

'Thank you, Miss Everdene.'

Bathsheba hurried away. 'Oh, what have I done?' she thought. 'He said that he loved me. Was he speaking the truth? I wish that I knew!'

7

'Keep Him Away From Me!'

Bathsheba saw Troy in the fields several times during the next few days. At first she was polite but cool towards him. But slowly, he found ways to make her smile and laugh. One day he asked her if she had ever seen a soldier's sword practice[74]. She had not, but she agreed that she would like to see it.

So, at eight o'clock that evening, she met Troy on the other side of the hill, a mile from her house. The evening sun shone on Troy's red uniform and bright, long sword.

'Now I'll begin the first exercise,' he said. 'First, there are four cuts to the right, then four cuts to the left.' His sword moved quickly through the air and he called out, 'One – two – three – four!'

The sharp blade moved so fast that Bathsheba gasped[75].

'Now I'll make the exercise more interesting,' he said. 'I'll pretend[76] to fight you. You'll be my enemy, but I won't cut you, of course. Stand there, and don't move.'

The sword moved like a bright light around Bathsheba. It made a sound like the wind.

First the blade went one way, then another way. Up, down! Once, it seemed to go right through her body.

'Oh, has it gone through me?' she cried. 'No, it hasn't!'

'I haven't touched you,' said Troy, quietly. 'Are you afraid? I promise not to touch you.'

'I don't *think* that I'm afraid,' she said, staring at him.

The sword moved again, and the light from the sun flashed on the bright metal. Soon, all that Bathsheba could see was a bright light flashing around her. Troy had never practised better than this.

'Your hair is a little untidy[77], Miss Everdene,' he said. 'I'll make it tidy for you.'

The sword went past her ear with a whispering sound. A small piece of her hair fell to the ground. She watched him pick up the lock of hair and put it in his pocket.

'I'll keep this forever,' he said. He came closer to her. 'I must leave you now.'

Then he kissed her softly on the lips. She was not strong enough to say or do anything to stop him. A moment later, he was gone.

Bathsheba was a strong, independent woman, and she was usually sensible. But now she lost her good sense. And she no longer had control of her own feelings. She was deeply in love with Frank Troy.

Bathsheba was like an innocent child. She knew little about men. And Troy's bad character was carefully hidden by his sweet talk. Frank Troy sometimes told the truth to men, but he always lied to women. Bathsheba foolishly believed that Troy was as good and honest as Gabriel Oak.

Oak saw what was happening. He was sad and worried, and he decided to speak to Bathsheba. He met her when she was walking home one evening.

'It's late, and I was worried about you,' he said. 'There are bad people in this area sometimes. And Mr Boldwood can't take care of you because he's away.'

'Why would Mr Boldwood take care of me?' said Bathsheba.

'Well, you and he are going to be married, and —'

'That's not true,' she said quickly. 'I didn't promise Mr

Boldwood anything. I've never loved him. He asked me to marry him, but I promised nothing. When he returns I'll give him my answer. It will be "no".'

Oak then made the mistake of speaking about Troy at that moment. 'I wish that you'd never met young Sergeant Troy,' he said. 'He's not good enough for you. He's clever, yes, but you can't trust[78] him.'

'Don't speak about him like that!' said Bathsheba. 'He's as good as anybody in Weatherbury!'

'Please, listen to me, Bathsheba,' said Oak. He spoke sadly but with deep feeling. 'You know that I love you, and that I'll always love you. I know that I can't marry you because I'm poor. But you are more important to me than my own life. Marry Mr Boldwood. You'll be safe with him.'

'Go away!' said Bathsheba. 'Leave this farm. I don't want you here any more.'

'Don't be foolish,' said Gabriel, calmly. 'You sent me away once before, but you soon needed me again. And you need me now. No, I'll stay because I love you.'

'All right, you can stay if you want to,' said Bathsheba, after a moment. 'But will you leave me alone now?'

She walked away. Gabriel watched her for some minutes, then he saw someone else on the hill. It was a soldier. Had Bathsheba been expecting to meet Troy? Gabriel Oak watched the two of them speak together, then he turned and went home.

Half an hour later, Bathsheba entered her house. Troy was going to the town of Bath for two days to see his friends, but Bathsheba was excited. Troy had kissed her a second time and his loving words were still in her ears!

'I must write to Mr Boldwood at once,' she thought. 'I can't marry him, and I must tell him now.'

After three minutes, Bathsheba gave the letter to Liddy to

send the next day. She told her maid about her love for Troy.

'People tell stories about Sergeant Troy,' Bathsheba said in a worried voice. 'But he *cannot* be as bad as they say. Liddy, you don't believe the stories, do you?'

'I – I don't know, ma'am,' said Liddy.

'Oh, how weak I am!' cried Bathsheba. 'I wish that I'd never seen Frank Troy! But I love him! You mustn't tell anyone, Liddy!'

'No, ma'am,' said Liddy.

The next evening, Bathsheba went to visit Liddy's sister. Earlier that day, Liddy had gone to her sister's house. She was going to stay there for a short holiday. She had invited Bathsheba to come and stay for a day or two.

Bathsheba had walked two miles when she saw Boldwood coming along the road towards her. He walked slowly and sadly.

She knew then that he had received her letter.

'Oh, it's you, Mr Boldwood,' she said. Her face was hot and red with embarrassment.

'You know that I love you, Bathsheba,' he said, slowly. 'A letter can't change my feelings for you.'

'I wish that you didn't feel so strongly about me,' said Bathsheba. 'Please, don't speak about it.'

'Then what can I say? We're not going to be married. Your letter was very clear.'

'Good – good evening,' said Bathsheba.

She began to walk away, but he stopped her. 'Oh, Bathsheba!' he said. 'There was a time when I knew nothing about you, and did not care about you. But after you sent me the valentine, I believed that you loved me. I believed that you wanted to marry me.'

'It was a cruel joke, and I'm sorry,' said Bathsheba.

'You're the first woman that I've ever loved,' said

Boldwood. 'And you *almost* agreed to marry me. Where are all your kind words now?'

'Mr Boldwood, I promised you nothing.'

'How can you be so cruel!' he cried. 'You gave me hope, and then you took it away.'

'I did not give you hope!' she said. 'You chose to *have* hope, sir. I can't love in the way that you love.'

'Perhaps that's true,' he said. 'But you're not the cold woman that you pretend to be. You have plenty of love, but you've given it to another person.'

'He knows about Sergeant Troy!' she thought.

'Oh, why didn't Troy leave my dearest one alone!' said Boldwood. 'Tell me the truth, Bathsheba. If you had not met Troy, you would have married me. Am I right?'

She could not tell a lie. 'Yes,' she said quietly.

'I knew it!' said Boldwood. 'He stole you when I was away! Now people laugh at me. I've lost my respect and my good name! Tell me, has he kissed you?'

Bathsheba gasped. 'Leave me, sir,' she cried. 'Let me go!'

'Tell me!' he shouted. 'Has he kissed you?'

She held her head up and looked straight at him. 'Yes!'

Boldwood gave a groan of pain. 'Oh, and I would have given *everything* just to touch your hand!' he said, bitterly. 'But you let a man like that kiss you!'

'Please, be kind to him, sir,' said Bathsheba. 'I love him very much.'

Boldwood did not hear her. 'I'll punish[79] him!' he said in a terrible voice. 'Bathsheba, forgive me for blaming[80] you. You did nothing wrong. Troy stole you away from me with his lies. But keep him away from me!'

Then Boldwood turned and walked away.

Bathsheba began to cry. She sat down at the side of the road and tried to think. She must keep Troy away from Boldwood until the farmer was quieter and calmer.

'Perhaps I should tell Troy that I don't love him,' Bathsheba said to herself. 'Then perhaps Troy will stop loving me. That would please Gabriel Oak and Boldwood. I need to see Troy. That will help me to decide. I'll go to him now!'

8
The Storm

Bathsheba went to Bath that night. She took one of her horses and a carriage, and she left her farm secretly. No one knew where she had gone. She stayed in the city for two weeks. News came back to Weatherbury that she and Sergeant Troy were courting. Gabriel Oak heard this news and his heart ached.

Bathsheba and Liddy arrived back at Weatherbury Farm on the same day. Soon after Bathsheba arrived, Mr Boldwood came to the farmhouse, but she would not see him.

Boldwood walked back to the village. It was now late in the evening. Suddenly he saw Sergeant Troy enter a house. The soldier had stayed in the house the last time that he had been in Weatherbury.

Boldwood waited for some minutes, then Troy came out of the house again. Boldwood went up to him.

'Sergeant Troy? I'm William Boldwood.'

'Oh, yes?'

'I want to speak to you,' said Boldwood.

Troy looked at the older man. He could see that Boldwood was carrying a big stick and he decided not to argue with him.

'What do you want to talk to me about?' he asked.

'Gabriel Oak and I know a lot about you and Fanny

Robin,' said Boldwood coldly. 'The girl loves you, and you should marry her.'

Troy turned his head so that Boldwood could not see his smile. 'I'm too poor,' he said.

'Then I'll give you fifty pounds now, and fifty pounds for Fanny's wedding clothes,' said Boldwood. 'And I'll give you another *five hundred* pounds on the day that you and Fanny Robin are married. Just leave Miss Everdene alone. She's too good for you.'

Troy seemed to think about this. 'I do like Fanny best,' he said. 'And you'll give me fifty pounds now?'

Boldwood gave him a small bag of coins. 'Here is the money.'

'Stop, listen!' whispered Troy. They could hear footsteps. 'It's Bathsheba. She's meeting me tonight. Wait here.'

Boldwood stepped back and hid in the dark shadows beside the house. After a moment, he heard Troy and Bathsheba talking. He could not see them, but he could hear their voices.

'Frank, dearest, is that you?' said Bathsheba. 'You're late. Was it a long, slow journey from Bath? I was afraid that you weren't coming.'

'You knew that I would come,' Troy replied.

'Frank, we're lucky! There's nobody in my house tonight except me. I've sent all the servants away. Nobody will know that you're with me tonight.'

'Wonderful,' said Troy. 'But I must collect my bag. Go home, and I'll come to you in ten minutes.'

'Yes, dearest,' said Bathsheba. And she hurried away.

Boldwood stepped out of the shadows. His face was pale with shock.

'Do you understand my problem?' said Troy. 'I can't marry *both* of them.' He laughed. 'But perhaps I'll marry Fanny. I like her the best, and you promised to pay me.'

'I'll kill you!' cried Boldwood. He jumped forward and put his hands around Troy's neck.

'Stop!' gasped Troy. 'Kill me, and you'll only hurt the woman that you love. I've already taken that woman to my bed and loved her. She must be my wife or she'll be ruined.'

Boldwood gave a cry and pushed Troy away from him.

'You devil!' he shouted. 'But – but yes, it would be a mistake to kill you. She has given herself to you, so she must love you very much. Oh, my Bathsheba!' He looked fiercely at Troy. 'Marry her, *don't* desert her. I'll give you money.'

'Keep your money, and look at this,' said Troy with a cruel laugh. He took a newspaper from his pocket. 'You're too late, Boldwood. Bathsheba and I were married a week ago. Here's a report of our marriage!'

It was a night at the end of August, and Bathsheba had been married only a few weeks.

Gabriel Oak came out of the barn to check the ricks of wheat and hay. They had no covers on them and he looked up at the dark clouds in the sky.

'There's going to be a storm,' he said to himself.

Sergeant Troy was now the manager of Bathsheba's farm. He had chosen this night to celebrate their harvest with a supper. Inside the barn, all the farm workers and their families were eating, drinking and dancing. Musicians had come from the village and there were tables of food and drink.

Troy was sitting at a table, drinking brandy and water. Oak had sent a young man to speak to him.

'Gabriel Oak has told me to give you a message, Mr Troy,' the man said. 'The shepherd says, "The ricks should be covered before the storm comes."'

A few minutes later, the young man came out of the barn with the answer, 'Shepherd Oak, Mr Troy says it will not rain.'

Inside the barn, Troy called to everyone.

'Friends!' he said. 'Tonight we have two reasons to celebrate. We're celebrating the harvest and also my wedding. I've ordered brandy and water for you all!'

Bathsheba put her hand on Troy's arm. 'No, Frank,' she said. 'Please, don't give them brandy. They've already had a lot of beer.'

Troy laughed loudly. He had been drinking brandy for several hours and he was already a little drunk. 'Friends,' he said. 'We'll send the women home. It's time that they were in bed! Then we can drink and sing as much as we want to!'

Bathsheba stood up and left the barn. She was angry. The women and children followed her.

Gabriel Oak went home and sat quietly, thinking. After an hour, he went to check the sheep. They were crowded close together in the corner of a field. The sheep knew that a storm was coming.

Oak hurried back to the farm and went into the barn. He needed help to cover the ricks before the rain started to fall. But he knew that he would get no help from the other men. Troy and the farm workers were asleep on the floor. They were very drunk and could not move.

Oak went outside again. The moon was covered by thick clouds and a strong wind was blowing. He pulled large rick-cloths over the first two ricks, but he had to make covers of straw for the others. He needed to attach bundles of straw onto the top of the ricks so that the rain would not damage the crop. Suddenly, lightning flashed across the sky. It was followed by a crash of thunder.

Oak found a ladder and the tools that he needed. Soon, he was working on top of a wheat-rick. It was difficult and dangerous work, but he did not stop. He pushed spars[81] into the bundles and attached them to the top of the rick.

Suddenly he saw someone moving on the ground below.

Bathsheba's voice called, 'Who's there?'

'It's Gabriel Oak, ma'am,' he answered. 'I'm up on the rick. I'm making a straw-cover.'

'Oh, Gabriel, I was worried about the ricks. Is my husband with you?'

'No, he's asleep in the barn with the others,' replied Gabriel.

She was silent for a moment, then she said, 'Can I help?'

'You can bring me the straw bundles, if you're not afraid to climb the ladder in the dark, ma'am,' said Gabriel.

'I'll do anything!' said Bathsheba.

She collected some straw bundles and began to climb the ladder. There was a sudden flash of lightning. It hit a tall tree not far from them and they watched it burn and fall.

'How terrible!' cried Bathsheba.

They worked together, as the lightning flashed in the sky and the thunder crashed around them.

Once Bathsheba almost fell from the ladder, but Gabriel caught her arm and held her.

'It's too dangerous,' he said at last. 'We must wait for the storm to go past.'

They climbed down to the ground and stood together. After half an hour, the thunder and lightning moved away. There was still no rain.

'I think that it's safe now,' said Gabriel. 'I'll go back up onto the rick.'

'You're so kind to me!' she said. 'Where are the other men? Don't tell me, I know. My husband and all the men are drunk in the barn. Gabriel, I must explain something to you.'

'Yes, ma'am.'

'I went to Bath to tell Troy that I would never marry him,' said Bathsheba. 'But he said that he had seen a woman more beautiful than me. He said that he would marry *her* unless I became his wife at once! Gabriel, I was *crazy* with jealousy[82] and – and so I married him!'

Gabriel said nothing.

'And now, please don't speak about it,' she said. 'I only wanted you to understand what happened. Shall I bring up some more straw for you?'

They worked on for a little while, then Gabriel said, 'You're tired. Go back to the house. I can finish this work.'

'Very well,' she said. 'Thank you a thousand times, Gabriel! Goodnight.'

At five o'clock in the morning, the rain came. Gabriel continued working. He smiled. Eight months earlier he had fought against fire in this same place. Now he was fighting against water. And he was here because he loved the same woman.

By seven o'clock, Gabriel's work had finished. He saw some of the men come from the barn and walk slowly past him. Troy was the only man who was singing when he came out of the barn. None of the men looked at the ricks.

Gabriel walked home and saw a man coming towards him. It was Mr Boldwood.

'How are you this morning, sir?' asked Gabriel.

'What?' said Boldwood. 'Oh, I'm very well. It's a wet day.'

'You look a little strange, sir.'

'Me? No, I'm quite well.'

Gabriel told Boldwood about his work on the ricks. 'Did you cover *your* ricks before the storm, sir?' he asked.

'No,' said Boldwood. 'I forgot about them.'

'You *forgot* about the ricks?' said Gabriel. He was surprised. 'You'll lose a lot of your wheat and hay after this rain.'

'Yes, probably,' said Boldwood.

Gabriel Oak stared at Boldwood. The farmer had changed. He was now even more unhappy than Gabriel.

'I was going to get married, Oak,' said Boldwood. 'You know that, of course. But things went wrong for me. I guess that people laugh at me in Weatherbury.'

'Oh, no,' said Gabriel. 'I don't think that they do.'

'But the truth is, Miss Everdene never promised me anything,' said Boldwood. 'I'm weak and foolish. I feel that it's better to die than to live.' He was silent for a moment. Then he said, 'Well, good morning, Oak. Please, don't speak about our conversation to anyone.'

9

The Lock of Hair

It was a Saturday evening in October. Bathsheba and her husband were riding home in their carriage. They were three miles outside the town of Casterbridge, and they were arguing about money.

'You mustn't gamble[83] on any more horse races, Frank,' said Bathsheba. 'You've lost more than a hundred pounds this month. It's foolish and cruel to spend my money like this!'

'Don't say that!' Troy replied. 'You're no longer fun to be with, Bathsheba. Why can't you be … ?'

He stopped speaking as a woman came towards them. They could see that she was very poor. Her clothes were dirty and torn and her face was thin and pale. When she spoke, her voice was weak.

'Please, sir,' the woman said. 'Do you know what time the Casterbridge workhouse[84] closes?'

When Troy heard the woman's voice, he turned away. 'I – I don't know,' he said.

When she heard him speak, the woman looked at Troy quickly. There was both happiness and pain in her face. After a moment, she gave a cry and fell to the ground.

'Oh, the poor thing!' said Bathsheba. She started to get out of the carriage.

'Stay there!' said Troy. He jumped down onto the road. 'Go on up the hill,' he ordered. 'I'll look after the woman.'

'But I can help you —'

'Go on, Bathsheba!' he said sharply.

Bathsheba and the carriage moved away. And Troy helped the woman up from the ground.

'How did you come here?' he asked. 'I thought that you were far away, or dead. Why didn't you write to me, Fanny?'

'I was afraid to,' she said.

'Have you got any money?'

'No,' she replied.

'Here's all the money that I've got with me,' Troy said. 'It's not very much, but I can't ask my wife for any more at the moment. Stay at the Casterbridge workhouse tonight and tomorrow. Meet me on Monday morning, on Grey's Bridge.

It's just outside the town. I'll be on the bridge at ten o'clock with all the money that I can get. Then I'll find you somewhere to stay. You'll be all right, Fanny. I'll make sure of it. Goodbye.'

Bathsheba was waiting for her husband at the top of the hill.

'Do you know that woman?' she asked Troy, as he climbed into the carriage.

'Yes,' he replied.

'Who is she?'

'She's not important to either of us.'

'What's her *name*, Frank?' said Bathsheba. 'I think that you know her name.'

'Think what you like!' he said.

They were silent as they rode the rest of the way home, and they did not speak very much the next day.

On Sunday evening, Troy went to his wife. 'Bathsheba, can you give me twenty pounds?' he asked.

'Is this for the horse races tomorrow?' she said. 'Oh, Frank! Do you *have* to go and gamble? Stay at home with me, your pretty wife. Promise that you'll stay at home!'

'I don't want the money to gamble,' Troy said.

'What *do* you want it for? I'm worried, Frank.'

'Don't ask too many questions, Bathsheba, or you could be sorry.'

'Oh, here, take the money!' she said. And she gave him twenty pounds.

'Thank you,' he said. 'I'll leave before breakfast tomorrow.' He took out his watch to look at it – and the back of the watch opened. Inside the watchcase, there was a lock of hair.

Bathsheba saw the piece of hair. 'That is a woman's lock of hair!' she said. 'Frank, whose hair is it?'

'It – it's yours,' he said.

'No. It's blonde hair,' she said. 'My hair is black. Don't tell lies to me, Frank.'

'All right, I'll tell you the truth,' he said. 'The hair belongs to a woman that I was going to marry. I met her before I met you.'

'What's her name?' asked Bathsheba.

'I can't tell you,' he said.

'Is she married?'

'No,' he said.

'Is she alive?'

'Yes.'

'Is she pretty?' asked Bathsheba.

'Yes,' Troy said.

'*Is* she pretty? With hair that colour? She can't be pretty!'

'You're jealous, Bathsheba,' said Troy. 'Don't be so foolish.'

'All right, perhaps the hair is pretty. Perhaps it is prettier than my black hair. But burn it, Frank.'

'There are more important things for me to think about,' said Troy. 'There are mistakes from the past which I must put right.'

'Mistakes?' said Bathsheba. 'What made you remember them today? Did that woman on the road make you remember?'

'Yes!' said Troy. 'There, now you know!' And he turned and walked from the room.

Bathsheba was miserable. Before she had met Troy, she had laughed at girls who fell in love with the first handsome young man who came along. Now she hated herself. She loved a man whom she could not trust.

The next morning Bathsheba got up very early and, as usual, rode around the farm. When she returned to the house, Troy had left.

After she had eaten breakfast, Bathsheba went outside again. She looked across a field and saw Gabriel Oak talking seriously with Boldwood. A few minutes later, Joe Poorgrass came along the road and they called to him. The three men spoke together for a few minutes, then Joe came to Bathsheba's house.

'Do you have a message, Joe?' asked Bathsheba.

'Yes, ma'am', said Joe. 'Fanny Robin is dead in the Casterbridge workhouse.'

'Fanny, dead?' cried Bathsheba. 'The poor girl! Why did she die?'

'I don't know, but she wasn't a strong girl,' said Joe. 'Farmer Boldwood is sending a wagon to bring her body to the church.'

'Joe, tell Mr Boldwood that *you'll* bring Fanny back to Weatherbury in my new wagon this afternoon,' said Bathsheba. 'Fanny was my maid. I must make the arrangements for her body to be collected. Before you leave, wash the wagon and put some flowers on it.'

'Yes, ma'am,' replied Joe.

'How long had Fanny lived in the workhouse?'

'Only one or two days,' said Joe. 'She arrived there on Sunday morning after walking from Melchester.'

Bathsheba's face became pale. 'Did she come along the road from Weatherbury last Saturday night?'

'Yes, that's right.' Joe looked closely at Bathsheba. His employer's face had become pale. 'Are you all right, ma'am? Shall I call Liddy?'

'No, it's nothing. Thank you, Joe. You can go now.'

That afternoon, Bathsheba asked Liddy questions about Fanny. 'What was the colour of Fanny Robin's hair?' said Bathsheba. 'I can't remember.'

'It was blonde – a beautiful golden colour, ma'am,' said Liddy.

'And was she was courting a soldier?' asked Bathsheba.

'Yes,' said Liddy. 'Mr Troy knew him.'

'Did Mr Troy *tell* you that he knew him?'

'Oh, yes,' replied Liddy. 'He said that he knew the young man as well as he knew himself. He said that the two of them looked very like each other. And —'

'That's enough, Liddy!' said Bathsheba.

Joe Poorgrass went to collect the body of Fanny Robin that afternoon. But on the way home, he stopped at an inn, where he met Jan Coggan and Mark Clark. All three farm workers began drinking. And some time later, Gabriel Oak found them in the inn. The three men were very drunk.

Gabriel, himself, drove the wagon the rest of the way to Weatherbury. But when he arrived at the church, it was late. Fanny could not be buried at night. So Bathsheba asked for her coffin to be brought to Weatherbury Farm. Fanny's coffin was put in the sitting-room of the farmhouse. Fanny would have to be buried the next morning.

When Gabriel was alone with the coffin, he looked again at the writing on its lid. He did not want Bathsheba to see the words: *'Fanny Robin and Child'*. With his handkerchief, Oak carefully removed the words *'and Child'*. Then he quietly left the house.

10

'You're Nothing to Me!'

Bathsheba and Liddy were going to their beds. Before Liddy went to her room, she spoke to Bathsheba.

'Ma'am, people in the village are talking about Fanny,' she said. 'They say that ...' She moved closer to Bathsheba and whispered the rest of the sentence in her ear.

Bathsheba's face became pale. Her body began to tremble.

'I don't believe it!' she said. 'There's only one name on the coffin.'

But after Liddy went to bed, Bathsheba went down to the sitting-room. She stared at the coffin. 'Tell me your secret, Fanny!' she said. 'I hope it isn't true that there are two of you inside this coffin. If I could look at you for a minute, then I would know. I must know the truth.'

A few minutes later, Bathsheba had opened the coffin and looked inside. 'Now I know,' she said.

Tears fell from her eyes as she knelt beside the coffin. Inside it, were the bodies of Fanny and the tiny child. Both of them had golden blonde hair. It was the same colour as the lock of hair that Troy carried inside his watchcase.

At last, Bathsheba stood up and got flowers to put round the coffin. She did not hear the front door open and close. She did not hear her husband come into the room.

'What's the matter?' said Troy. 'In God's name[85], who is dead?'

Bathsheba stared wildly and tried to run past him to the door. Troy stopped her.

'Stay!' he said. He held her hand and stood with her beside the coffin. He looked into it and did not move.

'Do you know her?' asked Bathsheba.

'I do,' said Troy. Then he went down on his knees and kissed Fanny and the child.

'Oh, please don't kiss them, Frank!' cried Bathsheba. 'I love you more than she did! Kiss me, too, Frank. Kiss *me*!'

Troy pushed her away. 'I'll *not* kiss you!' he said roughly. 'Fanny means more to me than you ever will! I should have married her and not you.'

He turned to the woman in the coffin. 'But in God's name, yes, my dearest Fanny, you *are* my wife.'

Bathsheba gave a long, loud cry. 'If she's – *that* – what am I?'

'You're nothing to me!' said Troy. 'Nothing!'

Bathsheba turned and ran out of the room. She left the house and did not come back that night. She returned later the next morning, after Fanny's coffin had been taken to the church.

'Is my husband at home?' she asked Liddy.

'No, ma'am,' said Liddy. 'He left early this morning.'

That night, Troy stayed in his room after Bathsheba ran out of the house. He waited miserably for the morning to come. It had been a bad day, even before he had come home and learnt that Fanny was dead. Earlier in the morning, he had gone to Grey's Bridge and waited an hour for Fanny. She had not come.

'It's the second time that I've waited and she hasn't come,' Troy had said to himself. 'Well, I won't wait any longer.'

He had gone to the horse races, but he did not use any of Bathsheba's money.

Now, as the sky began to get light, Troy left his room and went out of the house. He went to the churchyard. He found the place where Fanny would be buried later that day. Then he went on to Casterbridge.

When he reached Casterbridge, Troy ordered a gravestone[86] to be made for Fanny's grave. He paid for it with Bathsheba's twenty pounds.

Troy walked around Casterbridge for many hours. Then, at ten o'clock in the evening, he went back to the churchyard with some flowers. Fanny had been buried and the white gravestone was already on the grave. Troy knelt on the ground and began to plant sweet-smelling flowers around the grave.

When rain began to fall heavily, Troy went into the church and stayed there all night.

In the morning, he returned to the grave to finish planting the flowers. The rain had stopped, but there was mud[87] on the churchyard path. When he reached the grave, Troy saw mud on the white gravestone. And he saw something worse than this. The rain had washed all his plants out of the ground. They were ruined.

Troy stood looking at the flowers miserably. He did not try to replace the plants. After a few moments, he turned and slowly walked away. He walked out of the village and did not stop.

At Weatherbury Farm, Liddy took some food to Bathsheba's bedroom. 'Here is your breakfast, ma'am,' she said. 'We had some heavy rain in the night. And there have been some strange noises coming from the churchyard. Gabriel Oak has gone to see if the rain got in through the church roof.'

'Did Mr Troy come home last night?' asked Bathsheba.

'No, ma'am. Laban Tall saw him on the road to Budmouth earlier this morning.'

After she had eaten breakfast, Bathsheba went to the churchyard. Gabriel Oak was standing next to Fanny's grave. He was looking at the new gravestone. Bathsheba saw the words: *This stone was put here by Francis Troy in Loving Memory of*[88] *Fanny Robin.*

Gabriel looked at Bathsheba, but she was quite calm. She quietly told him to fill in the hole that the rain had made in the grave. Then she planted the flowers and cleaned the mud from the gravestone.

Troy walked towards the south. He had to get away from Bathsheba's house and away from Weatherbury. At about three o'clock, he came to the top of a steep hill. From there, he could look down to Lulwind Cove. The sun shone down on the sea and the bright sand. He was alone.

Troy decided to go for a swim. He climbed down to the beach and took off his clothes. Then he walked into the sea and swam out between two large rocks to the deeper water.

Suddenly, he realized that the sea was pulling him farther and farther away from the land. He remembered that this was a dangerous part of the sea. Several people had drowned at this place.

Troy could see the town of Budmouth, but he could not swim there, it was too far. He tried to swim back to the beach at Lulwind Cove, but he could no longer see it. Troy was tired. He could not swim any further. Suddenly, he saw a boat moving across the water. It was sailing towards a large ship. Troy waved to the men in the boat again and again. After a few moments, the men saw him and turned their boat towards him. Several minutes later, they pulled him out of the water and into the boat.

'Thank you!' gasped Troy.

The men were sailors. They took him out to their ship and gave him some clothes.

'We'll take you back to the land tomorrow,' one of the sailors said to Troy.

'Yes, all right,' he said. Then, after thinking for a moment, he said, 'Or perhaps I'll stay with you.'

On the Saturday after Troy left Weatherbury, Bathsheba went to the market in Casterbridge. It was her first visit to the market since her marriage and she went alone.

She was walking through the crowd when a stranger spoke her name. Bathsheba turned round.

'Are you Mrs Troy?' the man asked.

'Yes,' she said.

'I've got some bad news for you,' the stranger said. 'Your

husband is dead. He went into the sea and drowned.'

'No!' she cried. 'It can't be true! It —' But she could not say, or hear, anything more. She had fainted and fallen to the ground.

Suddenly a man pushed through the crowd of people and held Bathsheba in his arms. It was Mr Boldwood.

'What happened?' he asked the man.

'Her husband's clothes were found on the beach at Lulwind Cove yesterday,' said the man. 'Mr Troy must have gone swimming and drowned. Mrs Troy fainted when I told her the news.'

A strange look of excitement came into Boldwood's eyes. *Had* Troy drowned? *Was* he dead? He carried Bathsheba to a hotel. When she had rested, he offered to take her home. But after half an hour, Bathsheba decided to ride back to her farm alone.

Bathsheba told Liddy what she had heard. 'I don't believe the news,' she said. 'Mr Troy is still alive. I'm *sure* that he is.'

'How do you know?' asked Liddy.

'I don't *know*,' said Bathsheba. 'But I'd *feel* differently if my husband was dead. I know that I would.'

On Monday, there was a short report in the newspaper. A young man had been walking on the hill above Lulwind Cove. He had seen Troy swimming, far from the beach. But by the time the young man had walked farther along the hill, Troy had disappeared.

Later on Monday evening, someone brought Troy's clothes and his gold watch to the house. Bathsheba sat with his watch in her hands. She opened the back of the case – and there was the lock of Fanny's blonde hair.

'Frank belongs to Fanny, and Fanny belongs to Frank,' she said to herself. 'I mean nothing to either of them. I know that now.' She held the lock of hair in her hand. 'Shall I burn this? No, I'll keep it in memory of poor Fanny.'

11

A Promise From Bathsheba

For the next few months, Bathsheba lived quietly. She made Gabriel Oak the manager of her farm. Boldwood was very unhappy. He was no longer interested in his own farm and he did not often leave his farmhouse. So he also made Gabriel his farm manager. Then, very slowly, Boldwood began to hope again.

'Perhaps, one day, Bathsheba will marry me,' he thought. 'Troy is dead. Bathsheba won't think about marriage again for a long time. But I'll wait. And if she does marry again, she'll marry *me*!'

Bathsheba left Weatherbury and went to visit her old aunt at Norcombe. She was away for two months.

It was now late summer. Nine months had passed since the report of Troy's death. Bathsheba returned to Weatherbury at the time when the hay was harvested.

One morning, Mr Boldwood came to Bathsheba's fields and found Liddy working there. He spoke to the young girl.

'I hope that Mrs Troy is well after her time away,' he said.

'She's quite well, sir,' said Liddy.

'Does she ever speak about marrying again?'

'Never, sir,' said Liddy. Then she went on, 'Well, she did once say that she might marry again at the end of seven years. But only if Mr Troy doesn't come back before then.'

A few minutes later, Boldwood left the fields. So there *was* reason for him to hope. Perhaps, one day, Bathsheba would marry again. His love for her was deep and strong. He could wait.

It was time for the Sheep Fair at Greenhill. The fair took place in Greenhill once every year, and many people from Weatherbury went there. Visitors could play games or watch entertainments. And they could buy or sell clothes, drink, food and animals. Gabriel Oak took sheep from both Bathsheba's and Boldwood's farms. He hoped to sell the animals for a good price.

At the centre of the fair there was a large circular tent. Inside the tent, musicians and a travelling circus[89] gave performances. And one of the entertainers in the circus was Sergeant Troy.

After the sailors pulled Troy out of the sea at Lulwind Cove, he decided to stay with them. However, a few weeks later, Troy realized that he did not want to work on ships. But he did not wish to go back to Weatherbury.

'I don't think that Bathsheba will want me there,' he thought. 'We can never be happy together. We'll both think of Fanny Robin and how she died. And perhaps life on the farm isn't going well. Perhaps Bathsheba has less money now.'

So Troy had become an actor in the travelling circus. He acted as a famous highwayman[90]. In his performance, he rode a big black horse and wore a big hat, a long cloak and a thick black moustache.

And now, at Greenhill Sheep Fair, Troy suddenly saw Bathsheba. She was sitting with Boldwood and they were watching the play.

At first, Troy was shocked to see her. Then he saw how beautiful Bathsheba was – and he wanted her again.

'And she's still my wife!' Troy thought. He quickly pulled the cloak up to his ears. Then he walked out of the tent and into the crowd of people. He wanted time to think.

Later in the afternoon, Boldwood rode back to Weatherbury beside Bathsheba, who drove her carriage.

'Mrs Troy,' he said. 'Will you ever marry again?'

'My husband's body was never found,' Bathsheba said. 'He could still be alive.'

'Your husband disappeared a year ago,' said Boldwood. 'If he doesn't return, you can marry again after seven years. This is what the law says. If Troy doesn't come back, then you will have to wait for six years from now.' Boldwood's face was sad. 'You *almost* became my wife once,' he said. 'But that's nothing. You never liked me.'

'I did like you,' Bathsheba said. 'And I respected you too.'

'And do you like and respect me now?' he asked.

'Yes,' she said quietly. This conversation was making her feel uncomfortable. 'Mr Boldwood, I'm sorry that I made you unhappy. I shall always be sorry. It was wrong of me.'

'Don't worry,' he said. 'Don't blame yourself too much. But if you learnt that your husband was dead, would you marry me?'

'I don't know,' she replied.

'But perhaps one day?' Boldwood said.

'Perhaps,' she said.

'So after six years ...'

'Six years is a long time,' Bathsheba said.

'The time will pass quickly,' said Boldwood. 'Please, listen. If I wait for six years, will you marry me? It would put right all the wrong things that you've done to me. Do you want to be the wife of any other man?'

'No!' she said. 'I mean – please, I don't want to talk about this now. It isn't right. My husband may still be alive.'

'Of course,' said Boldwood. 'We won't speak about it, if you don't want to. But perhaps you can promise me this. Promise me that if you marry again, you'll marry *me*.'

'I'll never marry another man while you want to marry me,' she said at last. 'I can't say more than that.'

'So will you promise?' he said, excitedly. 'In six years time, will you marry me?'

'Oh, what shall I do?' she cried. 'I don't love you! I'm afraid that I'll never love you as much as a woman *should* love her husband. But it seems that I can make you happy with only a promise. So, yes. If my husband doesn't come back at the end of six years ... I'll think about marriage. I'll think, and perhaps I'll make a promise soon.'

'Soon?' Boldwood said. 'But "soon" could mean "never".'

'Well, perhaps I'll make a promise by Christmas,' she told him.

'Christmas!' he said, happily. 'Then I'll say no more about marriage until then.'

As the weeks passed, Bathsheba became very worried. One day, she was speaking with Gabriel Oak and they began to talk about Boldwood.

'He'll never forget you, ma'am,' said Gabriel.

And suddenly, Bathsheba told Gabriel about her worries. She told him about her conversation with Boldwood. And she spoke about the promise that she had to make at Christmas.

'And if I don't promise, I'm afraid that Farmer Boldwood will go mad,' she said. 'It's terrible! I don't love him, Gabriel.'

'And is it right to marry a man that you don't love?' he asked.

'Perhaps it isn't right,' said Bathsheba. 'Oh, I wish that I'd never sent that valentine card! I sent the card, so Mr Boldwood began to love me. Now he wants to marry me. I'll be punished for my foolishness. But am I free to marry him?'

'You are free to marry, if you believe that your husband is dead,' said Gabriel. 'Most people believe that Mr Troy drowned in the sea.'

12

Death at Christmas

It was Christmas Eve. Everybody in Weatherbury was talking about the big party at Boldwood's house that evening. Everyone from the village was invited.

Bathsheba was getting ready in her room and Liddy was helping her. 'I wish that I didn't have to go to Mr Boldwood's party, Liddy,' she said. 'I haven't spoken to him since September. I promised to see him at Christmas. But I didn't expect that the meeting would be at a big party.'

'But you must go, ma'am,' said Liddy.

'Yes, of course, I must go,' said Bathsheba. 'I'm the *reason* for the party. But you mustn't tell anyone, Liddy.'

'*You're* the reason for the party?' repeated Liddy.

'I can't say anything more,' said Bathsheba. 'Now, help me to put on my black dress.'

'Do you *want* to wear black clothes tonight, ma'am?' asked Liddy. 'Mr Troy disappeared fourteen months ago. You don't have to wear black for more than a year.'

'I won't wear a brightly-coloured dress,' Bathsheba replied. 'If I do that, people will say "She's not showing respect for her dead husband."'

Liddy finished her work on Bathsheba's hair. 'You look very beautiful, ma'am,' she said.

'Everyone will say, "She wants Mr Boldwood to propose marriage",' said Bathsheba.

'If Mr Boldwood *does* propose, what will you say?' asked Liddy, smiling.

'Liddy, I don't wish to talk about it! Now, give me my coat. It's time to go.'

In Little Weatherbury farm, Boldwood was also getting ready for the party. He dressed carefully, putting on a new coat which he had bought that day.

Gabriel Oak came to see Boldwood. After he had heard his manager's report about the farm, Boldwood asked Gabriel if he was coming to the party.

'I'll try to be here, sir,' said Gabriel. 'I must do a few things first. It's good to see you looking so happy.'

'Yes, I *am* happy tonight!' said Boldwood, smiling. 'Perhaps better times are coming for me.'

'I hope that you're right, sir,' said Gabriel.

'Will a woman keep her promise, Oak?' asked Boldwood. 'Not a promise to marry *now*, but in six years. Tell me, Oak.

You understand women better than I do.'

'Perhaps she'll keep her promise,' said Gabriel. 'But don't expect too much. She disappointed you once, and she's still young.'

'She never gave me her promise, the first time,' said Boldwood. 'If she promises now, then she'll marry me. Bathsheba is an honest woman.'

'Yes, sir,' said Gabriel.

'Now, there's something that I wanted to say to you,' said Boldwood. 'I know about *your* secret, Oak. I know that you have strong feelings for Bathsheba. But you didn't try to stop me courting her. Thank you.'

'You don't have to thank me, sir,' said Gabriel.

After Oak left the room, Boldwood took a small box from his pocket. He looked at a ring inside the box.

'This is for you, Bathsheba,' he said to himself. 'When you make your promise to me, you will wear this ring.'

Outside Boldwood's house, a group of men were talking.

'I heard news that Mr Troy was in Casterbridge this afternoon!' said Billy Smallbury.

'Perhaps it's true,' said another man. 'Perhaps Mr Troy didn't drown. His body was never found, remember. Does *she* know?'

'His wife? No, poor woman.'

'And it's best not to tell Mrs Troy,' said Laban Tall. 'Perhaps the story isn't true.'

At that moment, Boldwood came outside. As he went past the men, they heard him talking to himself.

'I hope she'll come!' he was saying. 'Oh, my dearest, my dearest! Why do you make me wait like this?'

A few minutes later, Bathsheba came up the path towards the house. The men watched Boldwood hurry towards her and take her into the house.

'Farmer Boldwood still loves Mrs Troy!' said Laban.

'Why are you so surprised?' said Billy. 'He never stopped loving her. But I wish that Mr Troy was dead. He's always brought trouble to Weatherbury.'

An hour after Bathsheba arrived at the party, she decided to go home. She went to get her coat from one of the rooms upstairs. Boldwood found her there a few moments later.

'Are you leaving so soon, Bathsheba?' he asked. 'The party has only just started.'

'I'd like to go now,' she said. 'I can walk home.'

'I've been waiting until you were alone. I want to speak to you,' he said. 'You know what I want to say.'

Bathsheba was silent. She looked at the floor.

'Will you give me your promise?' Boldwood said. 'Please, Bathsheba! Promise to marry me at the end of five years and nine months.'

'Oh, I don't know!' she cried. 'Please, let me go! I'm afraid! Perhaps Frank isn't dead!'

'Say the words, Bathsheba!' Boldwood cried. 'Promise to marry me! I've loved you more than anybody in the world. I would die for you!'

'All right,' she said at last. 'If Frank doesn't return in six years from this day, I'll marry you.'

Boldwood took the small box from his pocket. 'And you'll wear this for me?'

'What is it?' she said. She looked inside the box. 'A ring? No, I can't wear your ring! I don't want people to know about this proposal. Now, please, let me go home.'

'Please wear the ring,' said Boldwood. 'Wear it tonight, to please me.'

'All right,' she agreed. 'I'll wear it. But *only* tonight.'

As he put the ring on Bathsheba's finger, Boldwood's hand shook and his face was pale.

'I'm happy now,' he said and he left the room.

When she was calmer, Bathsheba followed Boldwood. She stood at the bottom of the stairs. The music and the dancing had stopped for a few minutes. A group of men were talking together in a corner of the big room.

'What's the news?' asked Boldwood. 'You men all look very serious. Has somebody got married or died? Tell me, Laban.'

'I wish that *somebody* was dead,' said Laban Tall.

Suddenly, there was a loud knock on the front door. A servant went to open it. After a moment, he came and spoke to Boldwood.

'Sir, a stranger wants to see Mrs Troy,' he said.

'Tell him to come in,' said Boldwood.

The stranger entered with his cloak covering half of his face. Some people had heard the news about Bathsheba's husband. They recognized Troy immediately. Boldwood did not recognize him.

Nobody noticed Bathsheba. She was staring at Troy. Her face was pale and shocked.

'Come and have a drink, stranger!' called Boldwood, smiling.

Troy walked into the middle of the room. He pulled his cloak away from his face and laughed. Boldwood recognized him at last.

Troy turned towards his wife. Bathsheba was sitting on the stairs and her dark eyes stared at him.

'Bathsheba, come home with me!' Troy said.

She did not move or answer.

'Did you hear me?' Troy said.

'Bathsheba, go with your husband,' said Boldwood in a sad, low voice.

But Bathsheba did not – *could* not – move. Troy held out his hand to help her to stand up. She was frightened, and she moved away from him quickly. He took her arm and pulled her towards him.

'Come on!' said Troy fiercely. Bathsheba gave a little scream and tried to get away from him.

Suddenly, there was a loud noise and the room was filled with smoke. Everyone turned to look at Boldwood. He was holding a gun.

When he had heard Bathsheba's scream, Boldwood's sadness had turned to anger. He had taken his gun, which was fixed to the wall, and shot Troy.

Troy was lying on the floor. He made a small sound, then his head fell back and he lay still.

Boldwood turned the gun towards his own head. But as he tried to shoot himself, Laban Tall knocked the gun out of Boldwood's hands.

'Well, it doesn't matter,' said Boldwood. 'There's another way that I can die.'

He went across to Bathsheba, and kissed her hand. Then he walked out of the house. Nobody tried to stop him.

13

'Marry Me!'

Gabriel Oak came to Little Weatherbury farmhouse about five minutes after Boldwood walked out. He went straight to Bathsheba, who was sitting on the floor beside Troy's body. She was holding Troy's head in her arms.

'Gabriel,' she said. 'Go to Casterbridge and bring a doctor. I'm afraid that it's too late, but go. Mr Boldwood has killed my husband.'

Gabriel hurried outside and got onto his horse. As he rode along the road to Casterbridge, he thought about Troy. Where had the man come from? Had Troy not drowned? Was he not dead at the bottom of the sea?

Oak rode fast. About three miles from the town, he saw a man walking along the road. It was Boldwood. He was also going to Casterbridge. He was going to tell the police what he had done.

Bathsheba ordered her farm workers to take her husband's body to her house. She washed Troy's body and dressed him in clean clothes. Gabriel and the doctor found her there when they arrived. Bathsheba was now weak and tired. Liddy put her into her bed and stayed with her.

Late in the night, Liddy heard Bathsheba whispering the same words over and over again. 'Oh, I am to blame! How can I live? Dear God, how can I live?'

In March, Boldwood was tried for murder[91].

Everyone in Weatherbury waited for news. But as they waited, they learnt more about the man who had shot Frank Troy.

After the Greenhill Sheep Fair, William Boldwood had begun to behave strangely. He had bought women's coats and dresses, then put them carefully into boxes. On the outside of each box, he had written the words '*Bathsheba Boldwood*' and a date six years in the future.

As time passed, Boldwood had become more and more excited. But he became less and less interested in his farm.

'His love for Mrs Troy drove him a little mad,' said the people of Weatherbury.

The judge at the trial also believed that Boldwood had become a little mad.

At last, Gabriel brought the news back to Weatherbury. 'The court has said that Boldwood *did* murder Mr Troy,' he told everyone. 'But he will not die. He'll go to prison for the rest of his life.'

As spring turned into summer, Bathsheba began to go into the fields again. Once more, she watched her farm workers working.

During the months since Christmas, Bathsheba had stayed in the house and had only spoken to Liddy. Now she began to be interested in the farm again.

One evening in August, Bathsheba walked to the village. As she entered Weatherbury, she heard singing in the church. She entered the churchyard, walked to Fanny

Robin's grave and looked at the gravestone.

First she read Troy's words: *This stone was put here by Francis Troy in loving memory of Fanny Robin, who died October 9, 18—, aged 20 years*. Then she read the new words that were written below: *In this same grave lies the body of Francis Troy, who died December 24, 18—, aged 26 years*.

Bathsheba went to stand outside the door of the church. As she listened to the sweet singing, she began to cry. She put her face in her hands, and did not see Gabriel Oak walk towards her. He watched her silently for a few moments, then she turned and saw him.

'Mr Oak,' she said. 'How long have you been there?'

'Only a minute or two, ma'am,' Gabriel said. 'I wanted to speak to you. I'm thinking about leaving England next spring.'

Bathsheba was surprised and disappointed. 'Where will you go?'

'I'll probably go to America,' said Gabriel.

'But everyone knows that Mr Boldwood made you a partner in his business,' she said. 'Everyone knows that you own the farm now. They expect you to stay at Little Weatherbury Farm. And what shall *I* do without you? Oh, Gabriel, we're old friends! You've been with me through the good times and the bad times.'

'I know,' Gabriel said. 'And I'm sorry. But I think that it's best for both of us if I leave.' Then he turned quickly and walked away.

In the months that followed this conversation, Gabriel only came to the house when Bathsheba was out. He sent reports to her about the farm, but he never met her. The day after Christmas, she received a letter from him. In his letter, Gabriel told her that he was going to leave the farm at the end of March.

Bathsheba sat and cried. She had expected Oak to love

her and help her forever. What could she do now? How could she manage the farm alone?

That evening, she went to Gabriel Oak's house. She knocked on the door and waited until he opened it.

'Mrs Troy!' said Gabriel. 'Please come in and sit down.'

'You'll think that it's strange for me to come here,' Bathsheba said. 'But I've been worried. Have I said something to make you angry, Gabriel? Something has made you want to go away. What have I said?'

'No!' said Oak. 'You *couldn't* make me angry, Bathsheba.'

'Then why are you going?'

'I'm not going to America,' said Gabriel. 'I've decided to keep Boldwood's farm and manage it. But I can't work for you, Bathsheba. People are talking about us.'

'What are they saying?' asked Bathsheba, surprised.

'People are saying that I have hopes to marry you one day,' said Gabriel.

'Marry me!' said Bathsheba. 'But it's too foolish ... it's too soon to think about that!'

'Yes, ma'am,' said Oak. 'It *is* foolish. I'm surprised that people can't understand this.'

'"Too soon" were my words,' said Bathsheba.

'I'm sorry, but you also said, "too foolish",' he replied.

'I'm sorry, too,' said Bathsheba. She began to cry. 'I only meant to say "too soon". Please, believe me!'

Gabriel Oak stared at Bathsheba, then moved closer to her. 'Bathsheba,' he said. 'If I only knew one thing —' he stopped and then began again. 'If I only knew one thing. Will you let me love you and marry you? If I only knew that!'

'But you'll never know it,' she said.

'Why?' he said.

'Because you never ask,' she replied.

Gabriel smiled happily and put his hands on Bathsheba's face. 'Oh, my dearest Bathsheba!' he said. 'My love, I —'

'Why did you send me that letter this morning?' she said quickly. 'It was cruel! It showed that you didn't care about me, and that you were going to desert me!'

Oak laughed. 'Oh, Bathsheba, you can be so annoying! You know that I had to be careful,' he said. 'People don't say very nice things about an unmarried man who works for a beautiful young woman. *That's* the reason that I was going to leave you and the farm.'

'Then I'm so pleased that I came to see you!' Bathsheba cried. 'I think about you all the time. I believed that you didn't want to see me again. Now, I must go.' Suddenly, she laughed. 'But, oh dear! Now I'm *courting* you, Gabriel!'

'Well, that's a good thing,' said Gabriel. He laughed. '*I've* courted *you*, my beautiful Bathsheba, for a very long time!'

He walked back to her house with her, but they spoke very little. They did not have to say anything. Gabriel and Bathsheba were old friends, and they understood each other well. Now that they had both spoken about their love for each other, nothing could destroy that love. And a few weeks later, they were married.

Points for Understanding

1

Why are these people on Norcombe Hill: (a) Gabriel Oak (b) the young woman with the dark hair (c) the gatekeeper (d) the fifty-year-old woman?

2

The author says that Oak is a man of 'good character'? Do you agree now? Give reasons. What do you think of Bathsheba's character? Why?

3

1 Why are these things important in this chapter: a ladder, water, buckets?
2 How has luck changed for Bathsheba and Gabriel?

4

1 Who was courting whom in this chapter? How and why?
2 Which people were honest? And which were dishonest?

5

1 What is Bathsheba's opinion of Boldwood at this time?
2 What is Gabriel's opinion of Bathsheba at this time?
3 Explain the word 'desert' in Bathsheba's note and why *this* message is important.

6

1 How has the relationship between Bathsheba, Oak and Boldwood changed? Give examples.
2 Why do you think Bathsheba is so attracted to the stranger on the dark path?

7

1 Why is Bathsheba no longer a strong, independent woman? What has made her lose her good sense?
2 'You can't trust him.' Who says this? Why? Who is *him*?
3 'You gave me hope, and then you took it away.' Who says this? To whom? Why?

8

1 Why does Boldwood give Troy money? What does Troy do next?
2 What things happen at the harvest supper which show the differences in the characters of Troy and Oak?

9

What is the importance of the title of this chapter?

10

1 'If she's – *that* – what am I?' Who is Bathsheba talking about? Why?
2 What happens to Troy after this conversation?

11

What promise does someone ask Bathsheba to make? Who asks her?

12

Who receives a shock at the party on Christmas Eve? Why?

13

Why are these things important in this chapter: (a) boxes of clothes (b) words on a gravestone (c) a farewell?

Glossary

NOTE: At the time of this story, British measurements were in *miles*, *yards*, *feet* and *inches*. 1 inch = 25.3995 mm, 1 foot = 30.479 cm, 1 yard = 0.9144 m, 1 mile = 1.6093 km. British money was *pounds* (£), *shillings* (s) and *pence* (d). There were 12 pennies (pence) in 1 shilling and 20 shillings (s) in one pound (£).

1 ***county*** (page 4)
the United Kingdom of Great Britain is made up of England, Scotland, Wales and Northern Ireland. Each of these areas is divided into smaller areas called *counties*.

2 ***arguments*** (page 5)
angry discussions between people who do not agree with each other.

3 ***guilty*** – *to feel guilty* (page 6)
Hardy had said unkind things to Emma when she was alive. He felt sorry about this.

4 ***buried*** – *to bury* (page 6)
when a person dies, their body is *buried*. It is placed in a wooden box – a *coffin*. The coffin is put into a hole in the ground which is called a *grave*. Graves are dug in a *churchyard* – the land around a church.

5 ***country area*** (page 6)
the land outside towns, where there are farms, hills, etc., is called *countryside*. The word is often shortened to the *country*.

6 ***celebrate*** (page 6)
when people want to remember a special time or event, they *celebrate*. They meet together to enjoy themselves. The meeting is called a *celebration*.

7 ***inns*** (page 6)
places where you can buy alcohol, food and pay for a room to sleep in.

8 ***cereal crops*** (page 7)
plants which are grown so that their seeds – the *grain* – can be used as food. Examples of *cereal crops* are oats, rye and wheat.

9 ***hedges*** (page 7)
lines of trees and bushes which grow around the sides of fields. *Hedges* stop animals from leaving their fields.

10 ***harvested*** – *to harvest* (page 7)
when crops have finished growing and are ready to eat, they are *harvested*.

11 ***corn exchange*** (page 7)
a place where farmers came to buy or sell the corn – the cereal crops – that they had grown.

12 ***hired*** – *to hire* (page 7)
when you pay a person to do some work for you, you are *hiring* that person. You are that person's *employer*.

13 ***good character*** (page 8)
a person who is brave, honest and works hard has a *good character*. A person who is dishonest and does not behave well has a *bad character*. People with *strong characters* often speak about their ideas and make decisions quickly.

14 ***wagon*** (page 8)
a heavy wooden vehicle with four wheels which was pulled by one or more strong horses. *Wagons* where used on farms and country roads to carry heavy things. A *carriage* was a comfortable vehicle which had four wheels and was pulled by one or two horses.

15 ***loaded*** – *to load* (page 8)
when something is very full it is *loaded*.

16 ***tollgate*** (page 8)
a gate across a road where you have to pay before you can go through it. The money you pay is called a *toll*.

17 ***flute*** (page 9)
a musical instrument that has the shape of a tube. When you play a *flute*, you hold it sideways to your mouth. You blow air over a hole at one end. At the same time, you move your fingers over holes along the tube.

18 ***giving birth*** – *to give birth* (page 9)
at this time, the sheep are producing *lambs* – their babies – from their bodies. Before the lambs are born, the sheep are *pregnant*.

19 ***stove*** (page 9)
fire is burned in this container to give heat. *Stoves* make a room warm, or they cook food.

20 ***beer*** (page 9)
a yellow or brown alcoholic drink. *Beer* is made from grain (see 8) that has been left in water and then dried, and plants called hops.

21 ***sheepdogs*** (page 9)
dogs that have been trained to guard and control sheep.

22 ***cowshed*** (page 10)
a building on a farm where cows are kept.

23 ***cloak*** (page 10)
a long loose coat without sleeves, that fastens around your neck.

24 ***recognized*** – *to recognize* (page 10)
know who a person is and where you have seen them before.

25 ***sidesaddle*** (page 11)
sitting on a horse with both your legs on the same side of the horse. At this time, women always rode horses on special saddles in this way. Men rode with one leg on each side of the horse.

26 ***embarrass*** (page 11)
make someone feel nervous, afraid, or foolish.

27 ***heart ached*** (page 11)
Gabriel Oak loves Bathsheba so much that he feels pain.

28 ***barking*** – *to bark* (page 12)
the sound made by a dog when it is excited.

29 ***best chance*** (page 14)
the best thing that he could hope for.

30 ***propose*** (page 14)
when a man asks a woman to marry him, he is *making a proposal of marriage*. He is *proposing* to the woman.

31 ***independent*** (page 15)
an *independent* person is someone who knows what they want to do and then makes decisions.

32 ***sheep's bells*** (page 16)
bells which were put around the necks of sheep. When the sheep moved, the shepherd could hear where they were.

33 ***chased*** – *to chase* (page 16)
run after something and frighten it.

34 ***deep chalk pit*** (page 16)
a large hole in the ground where chalk has been removed.

35 ***ruined*** – *to be ruined* (page 17)
loose all your money or power. Something that is broken or destroyed is *ruined*. In the nineteenth century, a woman who had a sexual relationship with a man who was not her husband was *ruined*. People thought that she had a bad character (see 13).

36 ***insured*** – *to insure* (page 17)
if you want to *insure* something, you have to pay an *insurance company* an amount of money. Then the insurance company will give you money if your property is lost, stolen, damaged, or destroyed.

37 ***debt*** (page 17)
an amount of money that you owe to someone. The bank had given Oak money to buy the sheep. Now he has to repay that *debt* to the bank.

38 ***farm manager*** (page 18)
a person who decides when and how work is done on the farm. The *farm manager* also gives orders to the farm workers.

39 ***regiment*** (page 18)
a large group of soldiers who fight together.

40 ***shepherd's crook*** (page 18)
a long pole with a hook on one end. A *shepherd's crook* is used to catch or guide sheep.

41 ***hay*** (page 18)
dried grass which is given to animals as food.

42 ***shy*** (page 18)
be nervous and worried when you meet someone.

43 ***guessed*** – *to guess* (page 19)
if you think that you know what is happening, but you do not know the truth, you are *guessing*.

44 ***rick of straw*** (page 19)
when a cereal crop is harvested, the stalks of the plants are tied together in *bundles*. When they were dry, the bundles were kept together in a big pile called a *rick*. Ricks could be made from crops of wheat, barley and oats. The dried, empty stalks of crops whose grain has been removed is called *straw*.

45 ***farmyard*** (page 19)
an area beside a *farmhouse* that is surrounded by buildings.

46 ***rick-cloth*** (page 19)
a large strong cloth that was put over a rick to keep it dry.

47 ***ma'am*** (page 20)
the short form of the word madam.

48 ***courting*** – *to court* (page 23)
have a romantic relationship with someone, especially someone that you marry later.

49 ***barracks*** (page 23)
buildings where soldiers live.

50 ***expect*** (page 25)
think that something will happen.

51 ***notice*** (page 26)
if you see someone or something clearly for the first time, you *notice* them.
The phrase is also used if you suddenly think that someone is interesting or looks nice.

52 ***annoyed*** (page 26)
upset and angry about something.

53 ***attractive*** – *to find someone attractive* (page 26)
think that someone looks beautiful or handsome.

54 ***valentine card*** (page 26)
a card that someone sends – on the 14th February – to a person who they love.

55 ***mail-cart*** (page 27)
a vehicle which carried people's letters and parcels between towns and villages.

56 ***man of honour*** (page 28)
a man who behaves well and honestly.

57 ***crest*** (page 29)
a raised part on the top of a soldier's metal helmet. *Crests* held birds' feathers or long pieces of animals' hair. Soldiers in some regiments, who rode horses to battles, had helmets in this style.

58 ***spurs*** (page 29)
short pieces of metal that someone wears on the heels of their boots while they are riding a horse. When the rider touches the horse with the *spurs*, the horse will move faster.

59 ***respected*** – *to respect* (page 30)
if someone is *respected*, people like them and think well of them. You *respect someone* because they are intelligent, or important. Or you respect them because they are kind and behave well. If you *show respect* to someone, you are polite because you think that person is clever or important.

60 ***disturbed*** – *to disturb* (page 30)
upset and worry someone.

61 ***sheep-washing pool*** (page 31)
each year, farmers wash sheep to remove dirt and insects from the wool on the sheep's bodies.

62 ***admire*** (page 31)
if you like the way that someone looks, works, or behaves, you *admire* that person. You are that person's *admirer*. The feeling that you have is *admiration*.

63 ***fiercely*** (page 31)
showing strong feelings of anger, hate, love, etc.

64 ***opinion*** – *want my opinion* (page 32)
your thoughts about someone or something is your *opinion*.
When someone *wants your opinion*, they are asking to hear your thoughts about that thing.

65 ***clover*** (page 33)
green plants that have small leaves with three round parts.

66 ***stomachs*** (page 33)
when an animal eats, the food moves from its mouth to its *stomach*.
67 ***swollen*** (page 33)
become bigger. The sheep have eaten a plant which makes them ill. Their stomachs are now very large because they are filled with air. This is giving the sheep great pain and they might die.
68 ***desert me*** (page 34)
Bathsheba is asking Gabriel not to leave her alone and in trouble.
69 ***riding-habit*** (page 35)
a jacket and long skirt that were worn by women when they rode horses in the nineteenth century.
70 ***silk waistcoat*** (page 36)
a *waistcoat* is a piece of clothing, without sleeves, that a man wears over his shirt. *Silk* is a beautiful, strong, soft cloth.
71 ***scythes*** (page 38)
long wooden poles with long sharp metal blades at one end.
72 ***Queen of the Corn Exchange*** (page 38)
women did not usually own farms and sell the crops. Troy thinks that Bathsheba is like a queen in a place where only men work.
73 ***wasted too much time*** – *to waste time* (page 39)
Bathsheba thinks that she has been speaking with Troy for too long.
74 ***sword practice*** (page 40)
soldiers were given instructions which told them how to fight with their *swords*. A soldier had to *practise* how to make cuts with a sword onto different parts of an enemy's body.
75 ***gasped*** – *to gasp* (page 41)
breathe in suddenly because you are shocked or surprised.
76 ***pretend*** (page 41)
do something or say something that you do not believe.
77 ***untidy*** (page 42)
an *untidy* person's hair and clothes are not in their correct places.
78 ***trust*** (page 43)
believe that someone is honest, kind and helpful.
If you believe that someone will say or do something which will hurt you, you *do not trust them*. You *distrust* that person.
79 ***punish*** (page 45)
do something to someone because they have done something wrong.

80 ***blaming*** – *to blame* (page 45)
say or think that someone has made trouble.

81 ***spars*** (page 49)
long, thin pieces of wood which were pushed down through the bundles to fix them onto the rick.

82 ***jealousy*** – *crazy with jealousy* (page 51)
if someone has something that you want, or does something that you want to do, you are *jealous*. *Jealousy* is this feeling of sadness and anger. Bathsheba thought that she was becoming mad because her feeling of jealousy was so strong.

83 ***gamble*** (page 53)
play games for money. Troy watches horses racing against each other. He pays to guess which horse will win the race. If he guesses correctly, he will get more money.

84 ***workhouse*** (page 53)
at this time, poor people who had no work, no home and no money had to live in a *workhouse*. They had to work very hard for food.

85 ***In God's name*** (page 59)
strong words that someone uses if they are shocked or surprised.

86 ***gravestone*** (page 60)
a large piece of flat stone that carries information about the dead person in a grave.

87 ***mud*** (page 61)
very wet, soft earth.

88 ***in Loving Memory of*** (page 61)
words that are written on a gravestone. The phrase shows someone's love for the person who is buried in the grave.

89 ***travelling circus*** (page 65)
a group of people and animals that travel to different places to entertain people.

90 ***highwayman*** (page 65)
a man who stole money and property from people who travelled on *highways*, or roads. *Highwaymen* rode fast horses and carried guns.

91 ***tried for murder*** (page 75)
Boldwood has killed Troy. He will be taken to a court and asked questions – *tried*. This is his *trial*. The judge and jury in the court will then decide if Boldwood meant to kill Troy.

Exercises

Vocabulary: meanings of words from the story

Put the words and phrases in the box next to the correct meanings.

insure shepherd disturb ruin annoy independent
barracks notice stove flute trust bark countryside
hire workhouse county debt blame celebrate
harvest respect character regiment tollgate
pregnant load embarrass propose

1		someone whose job is to look after sheep
2		a musical instrument
3		a machine that provides heat
4		the area outside towns and cities, with farms, fields and trees
5		to pay someone to work for you, or to pay for the use of something for a time
6		a region that has its own local government in some countries such as the UK
7		to do something enjoyable in order to show that an occasion or event is special
8		the activity of collecting a crop from fields or trees
9		the qualities that make up someone's personality
10		a gate across a road where you have to pay before you can go through it
11		when a woman or a female animal is expecting a baby
12		to put goods or crops etc. onto or into a vehicle
13		to make someone feel nervous, afraid, or stupid

14		the sound that a dog makes
15		to suggest a plan, idea or action; to make an offer of marriage
16		not depending on others for help; or not answerable to another government or organization
17		the state of something that is badly damaged or destroyed; the state of a person who has lost all his money
18		to pay money regularly to a company so that the company will pay you if something bad happens
19		an amount of money that you owe
20		a group of soldiers that can be divided into smaller groups; their commander is a colonel
21		a group of buildings where soldiers live
22		to become aware of something by seeing, hearing, or feeling
23		to make someone feel angry or impatient
24		to treat someone in a polite way because of their status
25		to interrupt, bother, or worry someone when they are busy; also to wake someone when they are trying to sleep
26		to be confident that someone is honest, fair and reliable
27		to say or think that someone is responsible for an accident or a bad situation
28		[historical] a poorhouse where people with no money were sent to work for food

Writing: rewrite sentences

Rewrite the sentences using the words in the box to replace the underlined words.

bark rent manage gamble disappear single
proposal trust harvest embarrass shepherd
pretty notice pond stare hire disturb
lie unhappy drown ~~kill~~

Example: 'Mr Boldwood has murdered my husband.'
You write: *'Mr Boldwood has killed my husband.'*

1 Gabriel Oak did not have a wife.

2 He looked after sheep.

3 'She's a handsome woman,' said the gatekeeper.

4 'I heard your dog making a noise.'

5 'Think about my offer of marriage.'

6 They put the cloth into a pool of water to make it wet.

7 'I do want to employ a shepherd.'

8 'Does anyone have a room that I can pay for?'

9 'I'm going to run the farm myself.'

10 She was annoyed because Boldwood did not look at her.

---

11 She was sorry that she had interrupted this quiet man's life.

---

12 Frank Troy did not tell the truth to Fanny.

---

13 He's clever, but you can't rely on him.

---

14 You mustn't bet money on any more horse races.

---

15 Bathsheba was miserable.

---

16 He went into the sea and died.

---

17 Bathsheba returned at the time when the hay is collected.

---

18 'Your husband vanished a year ago.'

---

19 This conversation was making her feel uncomfortable.

---

20 Gabriel Oak looked intently at Bathsheba.

Vocabulary: anagrams

The letters of each word are mixed up. Write the words correctly. The first one is an example.

Example: DRUBIE — put in the ground
buried

1	STANGERUM	angry disagreements between people
2	LITGUY	feeling shame for having done something wrong
3	LACERE	a plant that produces grain; a food made from grain
4	GHEED	a line of bushes or small trees that grow closely together
5	AGNOW	a vehicle, usually with four wheels, that was pulled by horses in the past
6	TEFLU	a musical instrument that you play by blowing into it with your mouth
7	VOTES	a machine that provides heat for cooking or for heating a room
8	PHOGSEED	a dog trained to guard sheep
9	DHOWSEC	a building where cows are kept
10	KALOC	a coat without sleeves that fastens round your neck
11	SHACE	to follow someone or something quickly
12	ROCKO	a long stick used by a shepherd; (it is also a slang word for a criminal or dishonest person)

13	RUNGCOIT	having a romantic relationship with someone, usually before getting married (old-fashioned)
14	CATVEATRIT	worth having; good-looking
15	NINVALETE	a card that you send to someone on 14th February, often without signing your name
16	NORHOU	a sense of moral standards and fairness; worthy of respect
17	SCRET	feathers on the heads of some birds; the top of a hill
18	RIMADE	to have a feeling of interest and respect for someone
19	NIPIONO	the attitude you have towards someone; the thoughts you have on a subject
20	VOCLER	small plant with leaves that have three round parts
21	NEWSOLL	increased in size because of injury, illness or flood
22	REDSET	to leave someone when they need help and support
23	ATACOWSIT	a vest with no sleeves, worn by men in the past
24	CHESTY	a tool used for cutting long grass or grain; it has a long handle and a sharp, curved blade
25	DROWS	a weapon with a short handle and a long, sharp blade
26	SPAG	to breathe in suddenly, often because you have had a surprise or shock

27	DENTREP	to behave in a way that makes other people believe that something is true which is not
28	GONERAVEST	a stone that marks the place where someone is buried
29	SICCUR	a group of people and animals who travel from place to place and give shows

Grammar: syntax

Put the words into the correct order to make sentences.

Example: The mother put the two women next to its calf.
You write: *The two women put the calf next to its mother.*

1 Bathsheba was learnt that the woman's name young Oak.

______

2 The young sheep had become excited and had chased the dog.

______

3 I'm wearing but the clothes that I have nothing.

______

4 He covered with the hay wagon and climbed into himself.

______

5 Suddenly around a noise he heard him and turned behind.

______

6 So the circus Troy had become an actor in travelling.

______

7 Suddenly with smoke was filled the room and there was a loud noise.

______

8 Now that nothing had they spoken that love could destroy about their love for one another.

______

Vocabulary Choice: words which are related in meaning

Which word is most closely related? Look at the example and circle the word which is most closely related to the word in bold.

Example:
countryside national (area) passport native

1	**character**	personality	letter	crook	table
2	**wagon**	dog	horse	load	cart
3	**toll**	road	gate	charge	church
4	**shelter**	sheep	protection	weather	hill
5	**lamp**	wool	cross	light	hay
6	**embarrass**	confuse	attract	compliment	encourage
7	**ache**	number	band	hurt	part
8	**plain**	simple	slope	hill	field
9	**propose**	marry	offer	reason	wife
10	**hire**	send	raise	lend	employ
11	**mug**	cup	fog	inn	beer
12	**barracks**	soldiers	building	regiment	sergeant
13	**maid**	farmer	load	servant	produce
14	**manage**	eat	drive	own	control
15	**annoy**	anger	notice	call	laugh

Macmillan Education
4 Crinan Street
London N1 9XW
A division of Springer Nature Limited
Companies and representatives throughout the world

ISBN 978–0–230–03052–7
ISBN 978–1–4050–8709–4 (with CD edition)

This version of *Far From the Madding Crowd* by Thomas Hardy was retold by John Escott for Macmillan Readers
First published 2007

This version first published 2007

Illustrated by Mike Lacey and Martin Sanders
Cover by Getty-Images/Store.

Printed in the UK By CLOC Ltd

with CD edition
2022 2021 2020 2019
12 11 10 9 8

without CD edition
2019 2018
6 5 4